MODERN ECONOMIC ISSUES

OTTO ECKSTEIN, Harvard University, General Editor

In this series the great public issues in economics are posed and put in perspective by original commentary and reprints of the most interesting and significant recent statements by experts in economics and government.

LESTER C. THUROW, the editor of this volume in the Modern Economic Issues series, is Assistant Professor of Economics at Harvard University. A Rhodes Scholar from 1960-62, Professor Thurow was a Staff Economist on the Council of Economic Advisers from 1964-65, and is at present a Consultant to the Council of Economic Advisers and Bureau of the Budget. He has contributed numerous articles to the scholarly journals, and is also the author of *The Role of Manpower Policy in Achieving Aggregate Goals,* to be published in the near future.

AMERICAN FISCAL POLICY

Experiment for Prosperity

AMERICAN FISCAL POLICY

EXPERIMENT FOR PROSPERITY

Edited by Lester C. Thurow

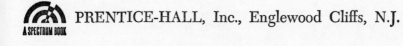 PRENTICE-HALL, Inc., Englewood Cliffs, N.J.

A SPECTRUM BOOK

CONTENTS

PART III   *Restraining Demand*

PART IV   *Future Fiscal Needs*

AMERICAN FISCAL POLICY

Experiment for Prosperity

INTRODUCTION

AMERICAN FISCAL POLICY

Lester C. Thurow

Since World War II, the real income of the typical family has risen 60 per cent, and real output has more than doubled. Although the absolute gains are large, the postwar record can be improved, for it is not as good as that of many of our European or Asiatic neighbors. On four occasions, recessions caused unemployment to rise to 7 per cent of the labor force. From 1958 to 1963 unemployment averaged 6 per cent; over the entire postwar period it has been 4.8 per cent.

The failure to make full use of America's resources has led to large losses in production and in standards of living. More important, severe social problems either have emerged or have been made more acute when many individuals and groups were told that the country was unable to provide them with meaningful work.

One of the central goals of economic policy is to improve the utilization of the country's productive resources without creating other problems, such as an excessive rate of inflation. To operate closer to capacity, recessions must be eliminated and the general level of aggregate demand must be held closer to the supply limitations of the economy. Since fiscal policies are the primary means for raising or lowering the aggregate demand for goods and services, they play a central role in achieving the maximum utilization of productive resources.

Decisions to vary government spending and taxes are the tools of fiscal policy. Changing government expenditures on goods and services directly affect aggregate demand, and varying tax rates or transfer payments alter private incomes and thus private expenditures. All expenditures and many taxes are designed to accomplish specific goals, such as improving the income of the elderly through the Social Security system; but fiscal policy is interested in how tax and spending decisions raise or lower the total level of demand for public and private goods and services rather than how they affect specific goals.

Although fiscal policy is by far the most important and powerful tool, it is only one of a large number of government instruments for influencing the economy. Policymakers can also affect monetary affairs through controls over interest rates and the money supply; incomes through guideposts for wages and prices, the war on poverty, and unemployment compensation; labor supplies with training programs and a more efficient Employment Service; the balance of payments with exchange controls and interest equalization taxes; and many other areas. By using a coordinated set of instruments, policymakers can come closer to achieving their goals than by using any one policy alone. If specific balance-of-payments measures can be devised to produce a viable international account, fiscal policies can be used to pursue full employment without worrying about hitting a balance-of-payments constraint before that objective is obtained. If other measures are not used, the flexibility of fiscal policy may be severely reduced. By itself, fiscal policy cannot achieve all of the country's economic goals.

Full employment, rapid growth, stable prices, an optimal income distribution, a sustainable balance of payments, and desirable economic institutions constitute standards for judging the effectiveness of aggregate economic policies. Unfortunately, both American and foreign experience indicate that not all of the goals can be achieved simultaneously. There is nothing in either the theory or practice of our economic system guaranteeing that the economy will achieve these goals. On the contrary, economic history is full of counter-examples illustrating the instability of economic systems when the government is not pursuing active economic policies. Even when a full set of coordinated policies is used in their pursuit, the standards do not necessarily represent a set of obtainable goals. Many factors can make the simultaneous achievement of all of the goals impossible, but the basic incompatibility in a system where private individuals have the right to set prices and wages lies between full employment and stable prices. Practical experience in every Western country indicates that there is no way to achieve maximum employment without encountering slowly rising prices.

If these goals cannot be achieved simultaneously, they have to be balanced to produce the maximum social benefits. Economists can identify the points of conflict and can outline the connections between policies and goals, but the primary job of weighting the relative importance of the different goals must be done by the public through their elected representatives. Value judgments, in addition to economic knowledge, are essential ingredients.

It is almost impossible to overstress the importance of these value judgments. Many of the essential differences in economic policies both between countries and between administrations result from the relative values attached to the different economic goals. To some extent, the lower unemployment rates and higher rates of inflation in Western Europe and Japan are a direct reflection of value judgments which lead to relatively more concern about unemployment and relatively less concern about inflation.

FISCAL POLICY: A TOOL OF CENTRAL GOVERNMENTS

Although state and local governments must make expenditure and tax decisions, only the federal government can have a fiscal policy. The federal government is the economic institution which can affect every part of the country and every American; but more important, it is the one unit which is free to set expenditures and taxes in relation to the needs of the American economy rather than in relation to its own balance sheet.

Whenever appropriate, the federal government can incur deficits, since the latter can be financed by increasing the money supply (a choice not open to the states) or by borrowing. When the deficit is financed by increasing the money supply, goods and services are purchased with budget receipts plus the newly created money. When borrowing is used, the extra funds are provided by the lender. The federal government is free to borrow, because its debt is internal. As long as borrowing is confined to Americans, the federal debt is merely Americans (in the form of their government) borrowing from Americans; as a group, they do not incur any net liabilities that have to be repaid in the future.

State and local governments cannot carry out fiscal policies for two reasons. First, since they do not control interstate commerce or their own exchange rates, they cannot limit borrowing liabilities to individuals within the state, and they cannot limit imports from other states. Second, in a national economy each state's propensity to import goods and services from other areas is so high that most of the benefits from a deficit-induced increase in demand would accrue to other areas. Since many of the benefits go to other states and since repayment of external debts represents a net liability, at some point the size of this liability prevents further state borrowing. State and local governments can run permanent surpluses and carry out permanent deflationary policies, but they are unable to provide a permanent expansionary impulse.

AN OUTLINE OF FISCAL POLICY

The strategy of fiscal policy is deceptively simple. If the economy is producing too little, government spending should be increased or taxes reduced to raise aggregate demand. If the economy is trying to produce too much, government spending should be reduced or taxes increased to lower aggregate demand. The difficult problems are ones of imperfect information and tactics. What is the correct level of production? Exactly when and how much should spending and taxes be raised or lowered? The techniques necessary to answer these questions are not simple and are constantly evolving as new and better data and methods become available.

Since the techniques used by economists during the Kennedy-Johnson administration have the advantage of making explicit many of the calculations and factors that are relevant in any method, they will be described in detail, although they are by no means the only possibilities. In using these methods or some alternative, one should always bear in mind the chance of error. The basic concern, however, is not whether perfect calculations exist, but whether the method under consideration makes fewer errors than do the alternatives.

Present methods can be divided into five steps:

1. Choosing an unemployment target;
2. Calculating the level of output (potential output) necessary to keep unemployment on target;
3. Forecasting what the actual output of the economy would be in the absence of fiscal policies;
4. Determining what changes in taxes or expenditures are necessary to close the gap between actual and potential output; and
5. Picking that combination of tax and expenditure changes which will close the gap and provide the maximum social benefit.

STEP 1: CHOOSING THE UNEMPLOYMENT TARGET

The full employment target depends on answers to four questions:

1. What are the social costs of unemployment?
2. What, if any, is the relationship between unemployment and inflation, and what are the social costs of inflation?
3. What is the minimum attainable unemployment rate?

4. How does society evaluate the relative costs of unemployment and inflation?

The Costs of Unemployment

The costs of unemployment are a combination of the actual losses in
production due to not fully utilizing every available man and the costs
in terms of human dignity (and the associated social problems) when
an individual is unable to support himself or his family. The direct
economic losses can be estimated by the associated reduction in actual
output. (Each percentage point on the unemployment rate means the
loss of approximately $25 billion per year in GNP.) The human costs
can be less easily measured, but they may very well be much more
important.

The human effects become especially important when we realize that
unemployment is not evenly distributed throughout the population. If
an unemployment rate of 4 per cent meant that each worker was unemployed 4 per cent of the time, unemployment would probably have
very few social consequences. If this rate meant that 4 per cent of the
population was unemployed all the time, unemployment would probably be an important cause of poverty, delinquency, broken homes, and
a host of other social ills.

Although neither extreme represents the actual situation, unemployment is very heavily concentrated among the unskilled and minority
groups. A national unemployment target of 4 per cent seems to imply
Negro unemployment of 8 per cent. Consideration of the social benefits
which would accrue from lower Negro unemployment might very well
lead to the goal of a 4 per cent unemployment rate among Negroes.
Unless other policies can radically alter economic institutions and attitudes, a necessary part of a 4 per cent Negro unemployment rate might
be a national unemployment target between 2 and 3 per cent.

The Relationship Between Unemployment and Prices

Both demand-pull and cost-push inflations are affected by the level
of resource utilization in the economy. As the economy moves closer to
full utilization of both capital and labor, alternative sources of supply
start to shrink. In some sectors demand becomes too great to be met by
existing capacity, and in other sectors market power becomes strong
enough to permit cost-push inflations.

Unemployment is a direct measure of the utilization of the available

labor force. Since it is also an important—if not the only measure of
the entire economy's resource utilization, economists have devoted ex-
tensive efforts to finding a stable relationship between unemployment
and price increases. No one denies that resource utilization affects inflation, but the exact relationship between unemployment and price increases is another problem. Reasonable connections have been found
between unemployment and wage increases (the Phillips curve), but in
the American economy similar results have not been found between the
prices of goods and services and unemployment. Perhaps the relationship
is unstable, or perhaps other factors, such as the distribution of demand
between sectors, need to be considered. In any case, no one can say
with certainty just what rate of inflation will accompany any given rate
of unemployment.

Historical experience indicates a wide range of results. Since 1950,
American unemployment has been below 4.5 per cent in six years.
During those years, the Wholesale Price Index rose an average of 2.3
per cent per year, and the Consumers Price Index rose 2.6 per cent per
year. The averages, however, cover a wide range of results. The Wholesale Price Index ranged from 11.4 per cent to minus 2.8 per cent; the
Consumers Price Index ranged from 8.0 per cent to minus 0.3 per cent.
In 1965 unemployment (based on American definitions) was 0.5 per cent
in Germany, 1.0 per cent in Japan, 2.3 per cent in Great Britain, and
4.6 per cent in the United States. The respective increases in consumers'
prices were 3.5 per cent, 7.6 per cent, 5.2 per cent, and 1.7 per cent.

With the exception of wartime, unemployment in America between
2½ and 6 per cent has been associated with slowly rising prices. The
rate of increase has not been fast enough to spiral to even higher rates
or destroy an efficient pattern of resource allocation, but even a slow inflation has some bad effects on income distribution. Small savers and
those with fixed incomes (primarily the retired) may find their real
incomes reduced.

The Minimum Unemployment Rate

Frictional unemployment is normally used as an estimate of minimum
unemployment in the United States. It results from individual mobility
between jobs and from turnover as people enter and leave the labor
market. Since labor mobility plays an important role in achieving a high
growth rate, zero unemployment is probably neither desirable nor obtainable. In the United States the usual estimates of frictional unemploy-

ment range from 2½ to 3 per cent with existing methods of hiring, firing, and prompting labor.

This does not mean that frictional unemployment is a constant which cannot be affected by public or private actions. World War II labor controls reduced actual unemployment to 1 per cent. Government policies, such as a better Employment Service, might be able to reduce the time necessary to find a new or better job. A period of labor shortages may encourage private business and unions to improve hiring, firing, and training practices. Private adjustments to meet labor scarcities may explain why other modern economies have been able to operate with unemployment far below estimates of frictional unemployment in the United States. Both Germany and Japan have had unemployment below 1 per cent (based on American definitions) without the wartime labor controls that would seem to be necessary here.

As with most other economic variables, there is no absolute minimum level of frictional unemployment. Achievement depends on what price society is willing to pay in terms of more manpower programs, slower growth, or less freedom to hire, fire, or quit work.

The minimum unemployment rate is a direct concern of fiscal policymakers if it is high enough to represent an unacceptable level of unemployment or if it has an influence on inflation. If minimum unemployment is above the desired target, manpower policies must be designed to reduce unemployment until the economic and social gains are equal to the costs of the policies necessary to accomplish the reduction. Minimum unemployment might also affect inflation if inflation depends on the excess capacity existing in the labor market. If desired unemployment were 4 per cent and minimum unemployment 2 per cent, inflation might be slower than if both desired and minimum unemployment were 4 per cent. In the former case some excess labor would exist and could serve to reduce the inflationary pressures. Thus even if unemployment targets are above minimum levels, social costs might be reduced by instituting programs to lower minimum unemployment.

Unemployment and Inflation as Alternative Social Costs

If we assume for the moment that unemployment and inflation are inversely related, policymakers need to raise or lower desired unemployment targets until the marginal social costs of unemployment and inflation are equal. If the costs of inflation are greater than those of unemployment, the unemployment target should be increased. If the reverse is true, the unemployment target should be decreased.

Although balancing the costs of unemployment and inflation is an unavoidable part of fiscal policy, there are other methods to mitigate the undesirable income losses of the unemployed or those who suffer from inflation. Instruments for redistributing income (principally unemployment insurance and Social Security) can help the victims of unemployment or inflation, but full compensation can occur only if the government aims for high employment and plans to offset any undesirable effects caused by the concomitant inflation. Unemployment reduces the total output to be divided; moderate inflation does not. High employment provides the extra resources necessary for redistribution to those who suffer from inflation, but stable prices do not provide the real resources necessary to compensate those who suffer from unemployment.

A program for high employment with an income redistribution policy to offset the effects of inflation could achieve both efficiency (maximum output) and equity (the desired income distribution). If economic policies were flexible enough to accomplish the necessary redistribution, however, they would probably be flexible enough to eliminate inflation before full employment was reached. When income redistribution systems cannot be established, the government is faced with the choice of lowering the incomes of those subject to unemployment or those subject to the effects of inflation. This is a difficult decision but an unavoidable one.

Even with effective redistribution policies, the unemployment goal is not zero. At some point the costs of further reductions in frictional unemployment will be larger than the benefits associated with lower unemployment. When this point is reached, the optimum unemployment target has been found.

The Actual Target

The Kennedy administration postponed the task of picking an unemployment target by choosing an interim goal of 4 per cent. Four per cent was far below the existing levels of unemployment in 1961, and yet it seemed high enough to avoid charges that it was unattainable. The Johnson administration also avoided setting a public unemployment target when the interim goal was finally reached in 1966. Instead it stated that economic policies "have now made prudent a reduction in the unemployment rate to a level below 4 per cent." Nothing forces policymakers to pick a public target, but there is no way to avoid selecting policies which will affect unemployment. No explicit unemployment goal was chosen in early 1966, but the policies actually followed in that year resulted in an unemployment rate of 3.9 per cent.

STEP 2: CALCULATING POTENTIAL OUTPUT

Theoretically, potential output is the maximum output that can be produced by fully utilizing an economy's resources. It depends on the size and skills of the labor force, the amount and quality of capital equipment, and the degree of organizational efficiency. In practical applications potential output depends on the definition of "fully utilizing." For fiscal policy uses, potential output is the level of production which would provide enough jobs to achieve the desired unemployment target given current resource-utilization practices.

Over a period of time, potential output expands as the size and skills of the labor force expand, as the amount and quality of capital equipment increase, and as the organizational efficiency of the economy improves. With rising productivity and expanding factors of production, the output necessary to hold unemployment on target one year is not large enough the next. The growth in output necessary to keep unemployment at the desired target level over time is the potential rate of growth. If potential growth is not high enough to satisfy the society's growth goals, additional economic policies (fiscal and other) need to be designed to accelerate it. By increasing investment, research, training, and hours of work, or by improving the organization of the economy, the "normal" levels of resource utilization and potential growth can increase without changing the basic unemployment target.

Three techniques are used to estimate potential output. (1) Empirical investigations of the relationships between past changes in output and unemployment attempt to determine exactly how large an increase in output has been necessary to hold unemployment constant. The growth represented by this increase in output is the potential rate of growth. By starting in a year when the economy is actually at the desired unemployment level, one can calculate potential output for any future period by simple extrapolation. (2) Direct estimates are made of projected trend rates of growth of labor supplies and productivity. Potential growth is found by simple additions. If labor supplies grow 1 per cent per year and productivity 3 per cent per year, potential output grows 4 per cent per year. (3) A formal mathematical equation is used to express the relationships between supplies of capital and labor and the total output of the economy (the aggregate production function). Inserting estimates of full employment capital and labor stocks into the aggregate production function, rather than the actual capital and labor stocks, enables potential output to be calculated.

FULL EMPLOYMENT MAN-HOURS

The supply of labor available for productive work at full employment depends upon population, the proportion of the population in the labor force, and the number of hours of work per day, week, or year. Each factor is subject to long-run trends such as the expanding percentage of older women who want to return to work and the desire for longer vacations, but except for population the factors are also subject to short-run economic conditions. When jobs are scarce, many people stay at home and do not look for work, since they suspect that it is unavailable. Since they are not actually looking for work, they are not classified as unemployed in recessions. Yet at full employment they would make a contribution to the total number of man-hours in the economy. The same sensitivity to economic conditions is observed in hours of work per week. As the economy moves to low unemployment levels, the amount of overtime expands and the average work week lengthens. In recessions overtime drops and the average work week falls.

To estimate accurately the full-employment man-hours available for work, both long-run secular trends and short-run economic responses must be considered. Simply averaging observed changes in the growth of man-hours provides some unknown combination of actual secular and cyclical effects and may provide a very misleading estimate of what will happen in the future. When cyclical and secular effects are distinguished, the potential growth of man-hours (based on the interim 4 per cent unemployment target) has almost tripled from 0.6 per cent per year to 1.5 per cent per year in the postwar period.[1]

The Full Employment Capital Stock

Private decisions to invest in capital equipment depend upon the utilization of existing capital supplies, the expected growth in demand, the quantity of funds available for internal investment, and the profitability of investment. Like labor force estimates, investment estimates must distinguish between secular trends at full employment and cyclical responses to an economy which is above or below potential. In periods of excess capacity, the need for investment might be very low even if the economy is rapidly expanding. As full employment is approached, investment may start to expand very rapidly in response to the sudden profitability of the new investment necessary to satisfy the demands for goods and services. Even at full employment there can be variations in investment needs due to changes in the growth of the labor force or to new innovations.

Full Employment Productivity

Productivity is an important element in the calculation of potential output, but it is not independent of the capital and labor supplies. Productivity is determined by the education and skills of the labor force (technical progress embodied in labor), the quality of capital equipment (technical progress embodied in capital), and the ability to organize and operate the men and machines in the most efficient manner possible (disembodied technical progress). The growth in each of these factors affects the total growth of productivity.

Productivity is subject to both cyclical factors and secular trends. When output falls, the growth of productivity decelerates, since overhead labor is not dismissed and since expectations of a recovery lead to decisions not to prune the production labor force to the maximum extent possible. When output rises from a recession low, productivity accelerates to very high levels, because the necessary overhead labor and some production workers are already on the payrolls. Estimating the growth of productivity at full employment requires a careful analysis of actual productivity to distinguish how much is due to cyclical factors and how much to the basic long-run determinants of productivity.

Unsolved Problems

Using the first technique for calculating potential output (estimating an empirical relationship between changes in output and unemployment), the Council of Economic Advisers estimated in 1961 that the potential growth rate was 3.5 per cent starting in 1955. With a more rapidly growing labor force their estimate was accelerated to 3.75 per cent in 1963 and to 4.0 per cent for the latter half of the 1960's. Since the economy reached a level of 4 per cent unemployment in 1966, the accuracy of the Council's calculations can be checked. Over the eleven years from 1955 to 1966 an average growth rate of 3.8 per cent proved to be needed to hold unemployment at the interim target.

The Council's methods were reasonably accurate until 1966, but they present some problems for future projections. The quantitative relationship used to make the potential output calculations was based on actual changes in output and unemployment from 1954 to 1961. If the same techniques are applied to the actual changes from 1947 to 1953, a potential growth rate of 4.3 per cent rather than 3.5 per cent results, even though the potential labor supplies were growing much more slowly in the early period. What rate should be projected forward to 1970—the 4.3 per cent modified for changes in the growth of population or the 3.5 per cent? Empirically the difference between the two rates is due to a much higher growth of productivity in the earlier period, but this merely moves the problem back to explaining why productivity increases fell.

One theory explains the higher growth of productivity as a backlog of unutilized innovations from the Depression and World War II; another explains it as a result of a period of full employment (unemployment averaged 4.0 per cent for the seven years) with the consequent encouragement to innovation and investment. The controversy would be of only historical interest except that it represents a significant difference when estimating the growth of productivity during a future period of full employment. The Council's estimates of potential growth could be accurate for a cyclical economy where the expectations and norm consist of high unemployment (the situation from 1955 to 1966) but inaccurate in an economy at full employment.

The second technique of adding the growth rates of the labor force and productivity suffers from the same problem. The pre- and post-1953 trends in productivity are very different. Which trend is to be projected into the future? The third technique of using a production function explains adequately the decline in productivity as a sharp drop in the rate of growth of the capital stocks between the two periods. The production-function approach eliminates the productivity problem, but estimates of potential output require projections of investment expenditures. Unfortunately, arriving at accurate investment projections is just as difficult as deciding which productivity trend represents potential productivity.

Looking forward from 1966 to 1970, potential growth rates will probably be between 4.0 and 4.5 per cent.[2] The exact estimate depends primarily upon the amount of investment that will be undertaken and its effects on productivity.

STEP 3: FORECASTING ACTUAL GNP

Forecasting actual GNP is an important part of setting fiscal policies. Since lengthy time-lags occur between the diagnosis of a gap between actual and potential GNP and the time when policies can close the gap, fiscal policy must be planned for some point in the future. Delays emerge because the President requires time to study the necessity of changes and to design an appropriate program, Congress requires time to consider his proposals and to change taxes and expenditures, the executive departments require time to put the changes into effect, and the rest of the economy requires time to adjust its spending decisions to the initial changes in government spending or taxes.

Instead of being designed for the current gap, fiscal policies must be designed to eliminate the gap that would be projected if fiscal policies did nothing. In peacetime, fiscal policy seems to operate with a minimum lag of nine months and an average lag of fifteen months between the initial recognition that something is wrong and the time when the corrective measures are having their greatest impact on the economy.

If policies have to be planned from nine to fifteen months in advance, forecasts of actual and potential GNP are needed for the same period. Without accurate forecasts there is no way to know the size of the gap between actual and potential GNP. Without this estimate there is no way to determine the appropriate changes in expenditures and taxes.

If forecasts of actual GNP are not accurate enough, three remedies exist. Efforts can be made to improve the accuracy of the forecasts, to reduce the time lags involved, or to improve the automatic stabilizers. Many proposals have been made for accelerating congressional consideration of presidential requests, in order to reduce one of the chief causes of delay. In 1962 President Kennedy requested that he be given stand-by authority to reduce individual tax rates by up to five percentage points, with the reduction in rates to take place thirty days after submission unless rejected by Congress. The reduction would have lapsed after six months unless Congress took positive action to extend the provisions. Similar stand-by authority was requested for up to $2 billion in public works. Congress refused to consider either request.

Fiscal powers such as those suggested by President Kennedy are much milder than those held by other governments (the English government can change any tax before gaining parliamentary approval), but there is no denying that these changes would diminish congressional power over fiscal policy. The relevent question is whether the diminution of congressional power is an appropriate price to pay for an economic performance that might avoid some of the losses associated with the delays in policy.

Errors in forecasting become most acute in war situations like that associated with Vietnam. GNP projections nine to fifteen months into the future become particularly risky when much of the economy depends on what happens to the war. When war emergencies arise, Congress has always been able to act rapidly. When economic emergencies are created by the cessation of wars, their agility is less certain.

Improving the techniques of forecasting provides an alternative to cutting fiscal time lags in the long run, but in the short run there is very little that can be done in this direction. Better forecasts depend on better knowledge of how the economy operates, and the policymaker has very little control over how fast economic knowledge is expanding.

Improving the automatic stabilizers provides a third alternative. The automatic stabilizers work through automatic variations in taxes and transfer payments to cushion changes in private incomes. If corporations pay a 50 per cent profits tax, a recession which reduces corporate profits by $1 billion is a net loss of only $500 million. The government suffers the other half of the loss. If a worker in a 20 per cent income tax bracket loses a job paying $100 per week and is able to collect unemployment compensation benefits of thirty-six dollars per week, his net income falls from eighty dollars to thirty-six dollars, not from $100 to zero dollars. As a result, his spending is less drastically pruned.

Several suggestions have been offered for making automatic stabilizers more effective, such as automatic tax rate reductions triggered by unemployment, or increases in the size of transfer payments. Both items would more fully offset income changes and the induced variations in spending.

The automatic stabilizers can easily be altered to improve their ability to reduce income declines during recessions, but they are of less use when a gap between potential and actual output arises because the economy is growing too fast or too slowly. Discretionary policies can be much more sensitive to the needs of the economy than automatic stabilizers which depend on some trigger mechanisms. Forecasts and the resulting discretionary policies are fallible, but they are much more accurate and sensitive than trigger mechanisms and the resulting automatic stabilizers.

STEP 4: CLOSING THE GAP BETWEEN ACTUAL AND POTENTIAL GNP

If actual GNP does not equal potential GNP, fiscal instruments must be used either to raise or to lower actual GNP until the two are equal. The projected difference between actual and potential GNP is the gap which must be closed, but it cannot be closed by simply increasing or decreasing taxes and expenditures by the amount of the gap. Changes in tax rates and government expenditures induce further changes in private incomes and expenditures which must be considered.

If fiscal policies lead to higher private incomes, consumption expenditures increase as a result. Higher private expenditures create, in turn, higher incomes for the groups producing the desired private goods. The chain of rising expenditures continues over a long period of time, but the magnitude of the increases quickly becomes small, since part of every increase in incomes is siphoned off into corporate profits, savings, taxes, and imports. In the American economy the final increase in expenditures is two to two and one-half times as large as the initial change in expenditures or taxes. This is called the multiplier effect.

Investment spending is also subject to induced effects. If idle plant and equipment exist, the induced effects may be minor, but when operating rates approach capacity, additional orders from government expenditures or from induced private demand may lead to a decision to expand production facilities in order to meet demand. This is called the accelerator effect.

A third source of induced spending comes from state and local governments. Increased production and higher private incomes increase state revenues and may increase demands for state and municipal services.

Both the magnitude of the final increases in consumption, investment, and government spending and the way in which these changes are spread over time become important in setting fiscal policy. Effects occurring two years in the future do not help close a gap expected to exist one year in the future. In eliminating the gap between actual and potential GNP, the challenge is to determine the initial change in government expenditures and/or taxes which is just large enough to induce the desired changes in consumption, investment, and state and local spending which will jointly close the gap at each point in time.

STEP 5: PICKING THE CORRECT COMBINATION OF EXPENDITURE AND TAX POLICIES

Theoretically the choice between using taxes or expenditures to close a gap is clear. Government spending should be set so that, given the level of potential output, the marginal benefit from public expenditures is equal to the marginal benefit from private spending for consumption or investment. If the marginal benefits from public expenditures are larger, public spending needs to be increased. If the marginal benefits are smaller, public spending must be reduced and private spending enlarged.

To maintain an economy at full employment, higher government spending would have to be combined with higher taxes, and lower expenditures would have to be combined with lower taxes. In an economy short of full employment a combination of expenditures and/or tax reductions can be used both to raise aggregate demand and to improve the balance between public and private spending. If the marginal benefit of public expenditures were much greater than the marginal benefit of private expenditures, closing a gap might require the combination of larger public expenditures and tax increases. Initial changes in fiscal policy may be restricted to public expenditures, but the induced increases occur primarily in private expenditures. If the initial increase in public spending is not large enough to maintain an equilibrium in marginal benefits, a tax increase may be necessary to permit an even larger increase in public expenditures.

The theoretical choice between tax or expenditure instruments is straightforward, but the practical problems are more arduous. First, it is difficult to measure the relative marginal benefits from public and private spending. Second, the political feasibility of obtaining civilian expenditures from Congress may very well depend on whether fiscal policies are designed to contract or expand the economy. Congress may be willing to devote part of the increment of a growing economy to public expenditures, but unwilling to lower private expenditures to facilitate raising public ones. The debate between tax reductions and expenditure increases may be politically important even though economic theory provides a clear method for settling the issue.

THE TOOLS FOR ANALYZING FISCAL POLICY

The Full Employment Surplus

To determine what fiscal policy the federal government has been following, analysis must go beyond actual changes in tax revenues and expenditures. All tax revenues and some expenditures (unemployment compensation, welfare payments) depend upon the level of output in the economy. Thus as an economy moves into a recession, falling tax revenues (and a rising deficit) do not necessarily indicate that active steps are being taken to raise demand. The effects may merely be part of the automatic stabilizers which help to prevent an economy from heading into a severe depression or a spiraling inflation.

One simple correction for these induced changes is to calculate budget receipts and expenditures on the assumption that the economy is continually at full employment. Using the national income accounts budget, this calculation yields the "full employment surplus or deficit." Changes in the full employment surplus indicate whether the government is moving toward a more or less restrictive policy. If government savings increase (a rising full employment surplus or a falling full employment deficit), the aggregate demand for goods and services falls unless some other sector offsets the change by increasing its own demand. If government savings decrease (a falling full employment surplus or a rising full employment deficit), the aggregate demand for goods and services rises. By increasing or decreasing savings plans, the government increases or decreases its deflationary impact.

By itself, the level of the full employment surplus cannot be used to determine whether the federal government is on balance, a constrictive or expansionary force in the economy. Whether or not the federal government is expanding demand with its expenditure programs by more than it is constricting demand with its tax programs depends upon the level of the federal budget and its composition (both on the tax and expenditure sides) as well as the level of the full employment surplus. If some tax receipts come out of private savings, a balanced budget can lead to a net stimulation of aggregate demand, since government demand increases by more than the reduction in private demand. The composition of taxes and expenditures is important since all taxes and expenditures do not have the same effects on demand. Taxes differ in how much they affect savings, and expenditures may have very different effects upon aggregate demand. Transfer payments have no direct effect and rely entirely upon induced effects on private expenditures while expenditures on goods and services, in addition to their induced impact on private spending, directly expand demand.

Fiscal policy becomes more and more deflationary as potential output expands over time if neither tax rates nor expenditure programs are altered. Tax receipts expand with the growing economy, but expenditures do not. As a result the full employment surplus rises. Since the government's potential savings are expanding, the private sector must continually expand its borrowing of these savings if the economy is to operate at full employment. The resultant increase in deflationary pressures is "fiscal drag." The need to offset fiscal drag by cutting taxes or increasing expenditure in order to remain at full employment is the "fiscal dividend." Taxes must be reduced or expenditures increased if the economy is to remain at full employment.

A neutral fiscal policy which neither expands nor contracts the economy could be designed, but neutrality in no sense implies a desirable goal. The only goal is that surplus or deficit which holds the economy at full employment. If potential GNP is larger than actual GNP, the full employment surplus should be reduced by cutting taxes or by increasing expenditure by a large enough amount to offset the normal growth in the full employment surplus and to achieve the desired reduction. If actual GNP is above potential GNP the full employment surplus needs to be increased. If the desired expansion is larger than that which will occur with passive fiscal policies, active measures need to be taken to raise taxes or to cut expenditures.

The Optimal Full Employment Surplus

The decision to increase or decrease the full employment surplus depends on whether actual GNP must be contracted or expanded, but the optimum level at full employment depends on the relationship between planned private investment and planned private saving. If private investment plans are larger than private savings plans, government fiscal policies need to generate a surplus (savings) to provide the needed goods and services. If private saving plans are larger than private investment plans, the government needs to generate a deficit to use the resources which the excess savings represent.

Since private decisions change in relation to investment and consumption opportunities, the decision to achieve a surplus or deficit of any given amount is not a decision that can or should be made for a long period of time. At frequent intervals, fiscal policies must be revised to account for changes in the forces determining private savings and investment.

The fiscal policies necessary to close a gap between actual and potential GNP are also not necessarily the policies needed for *keeping* it closed. When actual GNP is below potential GNP, idle capacity may lead to very small investment expenditures even though the economy is growing rapidly. If private savings plans are higher than private investment plans, a full employment deficit may be needed to offset private savings as the economy moves to full employment. Once full employment is reached, however, private investment expenditures may expand very rapidly. With strong private investment, fiscal policies must gradually shift toward a higher full employment surplus or lower deficit to prevent the economy from moving above potential levels.

Although the full employment surplus is not a measure that can be used to set the details of fiscal policy because different taxes and different expenditures have different induced effects on the private economy, it does provide a useful tool for analyzing the broad thrust of fiscal policy. Despite its limitations, it is the best single measure of what fiscal actions the federal government is taking to depress or stimulate the economy.

APPLYING THE TOOLS OF FISCAL ANALYSIS

1955-1960

In the wake of the 1954 recession and on a surge of spending for housing, automobiles, and inventories, GNP grew by 7.6 per cent in 1955 and unemployment fell to 4 per cent by mid-year. With strong private demands for goods and services, full employment (based on the 4 per cent goal) was compatible with a full employment (and actual) surplus

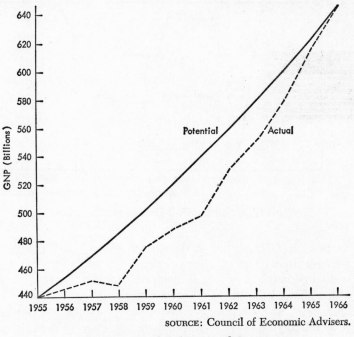

SOURCE: Council of Economic Advisers.

Chart I. Actual and Potential Output

of $4 billion. (See Charts I and II) The demand for housing and auto-
mobiles was unsustainable since private incomes were growing at much
slower rates. But when demand did start to fall at the end of 1955, business expectations of a future boom offset the effects by rapidly expanding demand for private fixed investment. From 1955 to 1956 the rise in
plant and equipment expenditures accounted for over 40 per cent of the

SOURCE: Council of Economic Advisers.

***Chart II.** Actual and Full Employment Surpluses*

total increase in GNP, although the growth of real GNP dropped to 2
per cent because of a lack of aggregate demand in other sectors.

The slower growth in aggregate demand was reinforced by fiscal policies which allowed the full employment surplus to grow from $4 billion
to $6 billion in 1956. Despite an increase in government expenditures of
almost $4 billion, the latent strength of passive fiscal policies moved the
government to a slightly more deflationary position. Unemployment

did not rise substantially because expectations of a future boom also lead to labor hoarding even though labor was not needed for current production.

From mid-1956 to mid-1957, defense purchases resulting from the Hungarian rebellion, the Suez crisis, and Sputnik rose fast enough to hold the full employment surplus constant at $6 billion. With a continuing boom in plant and equipment expenditures coupled with expectations of a future rise in demand, unemployment remained essentially constant.

By 1957, however, the investment expenditures of the previous year were starting to result in additional productive capacity. Combined with a slow growth of consumption demands, capacity utilization rates began to fall. The natural reaction was a decline in new investment expenditures. When the increases in federal defense expenditures ceased in mid-1957, aggregate demand started to fall and the economy headed into the 1958 recession. Unemployment quickly rose from 4.2 per cent to 7.5 per cent. In early 1957 a $6 billion full employment surplus was compatible with stable unemployment because of military spending, strong investment expenditures, and the expectation of a future industrial boom, but it was far from compatible with full employment when the three factors evaporated in late 1957. Combined with the Federal Reserve Board's decision to tighten credit conditions, economic policies were much too deflationary. Actual GNP fell at an annual rate of almost 8 per cent from the third quarter of 1957 to the first quarter of 1958.

In 1958 a combination of automatic stabilizers and discretionary actions increased government spending by more than $9 billion, offsetting the normal growth in the full employment surplus and causing a modest reduction to $3 billion. With manufacturing operations at 73 per cent of capacity, with the expectations of a future boom evaporated, and with the economy in the midst of a recession, a full employment surplus of $3 billion (a level more than compatible with full employment in 1955) was probably not low enough to close the gap between actual and potential output.

While a $3 billion surplus might not have been low enough to eliminate the gap which had developed, it was large enough to reduce the gap, and the economy started to expand. Whether a $3 billion surplus would have led to full employment is a moot point since the recovery was aborted by policies which allowed fiscal drag to increase the full employment surplus to $7 billion in 1959 and to $12 billion in 1960. Passive fiscal policies, active presidential opposition to expenditure increases, and higher Social Security and federal gasoline taxes led to an increasingly deflationary fiscal policy. Tight monetary policies ended the housing boom started by the low interest rates of 1958. The economy headed into another recession in the third quarter of 1960 and unemployment quickly rose from 5 to over 7 per cent.

The 1958 recession occurred when fiscal policymakers made an error of omission and failed to offset changes in private expectations and spending plans. In 1960-61 the error was one of commission. The deflationary impact of the government rose and private spending plans were simply not strong enough to offset potential government savings of $12 billion. With a deflationary impact of this magnitude, demand fell.

Fiscal policies became very restrictive after 1958 for three reasons:

1. The administration wanted to prevent a recurrence of the 1955-57 inflation;
2. It wanted to improve the balance of payments; and
3. It wanted to balance the administrative budget.

While the choice of goals can only be faulted with alternative value judgments, questions can be raised as to whether fiscal policies were the proper instruments for achieving these goals. A higher rate of unemployment might have been necessary to reduce inflation, but the same reduction in inflation could probably have been accomplished with unemployment rates of less than 5.5 per cent and certainly without the 1960-61 recession.

In the American economy, fiscal policy is a very expensive method of improving the balance of payments. Given a very small marginal propensity to import, a small reduction in imports requires a large reduction in production. When this is combined with capital outflows which are sensitive to rates of return on investment (American investment abroad increases when domestic returns fall during recessions), improvements in the balance of payments may require very large changes in output and unemployment.

1961-1966

The new administration's value judgments led to a different ordering of economic goals and to some new techniques for setting economic policies. Low unemployment and rapid growth (to compete with the Russians) became the major goals. The relative importance of inflation was reduced and an attempt was made to deal with it independently through the guideposts for wages and prices. The balance of payments was to become the province of monetary controls and specific measures (such as the interest equalization tax) rather than fiscal policy; the virtues of the balanced administrative budget were to become economic myths. The new administration intended a revolution in economic values, but congressional interests in the old goals meant that actual policies were not radically different.

The new administration inherited an economy with unemployment near 7 per cent and manufacturing operating rates at 77 per cent of capacity. Expenditure increases of $17 billion from 1960 to 1962 reduced the full employment surplus from $12 billion to less than $7 billion, but these increases were not motivated by fiscal analysis. Most of the increases came in military and space expenditures that would have been undertaken under any administration. The one positive action was to refrain from asking for a tax increase to cover the additional spending. Whatever its genesis, a lower full employment surplus did expand demand and reduce unemployment to 5.5 percent in 1962, increasing the rate of growth to 6.5 percent from 1961 to 1962.

To achieve a higher potential rate of growth, the first active fiscal measures of the new administration were designed to expand investment. New depreciation guidelines and the 7 per cent investment tax credit were designed to increase the quantity of internal funds available for investment and to increase the profitability of investment. In addition to the carrot of higher returns, a stick was provided by a provision that the extra funds would be lost if they were not in fact reinvested before a suitable interval had elapsed (a provision rescinded in 1965 before anyone was penalized). The fiscal strategy was to engineer an investment boom based on these two measures that would carry the economy to full employment while increasing the rate of growth.

In 1962 operating rates reached 86 per cent of capacity, but were below the desired levels of 92 to 93 per cent. In this environment the attempt to stimulate investment failed. Investment simply did not respond to the new measures. As a per cent of GNP, nonresidential fixed investment remained constant at 9.4 per cent from 1962 to 1963.

Given the relative stagnation in investment spending and a deceleration in expenditure increases, the full employment surplus rose from $7 billion in 1962 to almost $11 billion in 1963. Unemployment rose slightly and the growth of GNP fell to 4 per cent. Government policies were simply too deflationary to permit the economy to move to lower unemployment rates. By early 1963 the administration was convinced that investment was not going to respond as strongly as it had hoped and that other measures were needed. They recommended a general personal and corporate tax reduction. Congressional hesitation to pass the measure due to fears about deficits, desires to cut spending, and fights over the concomitant tax reforms meant that the tax cut was not passed until early 1964 under President Johnson.

After it had passed, the resultant $13 billion cut in taxes (at annual rates) plus the government expenditure increases reduced the full employment surplus from $11 billion to $4 billion in 1964. With a large fiscal stimulus to demand, output rose 5.3 per cent and unemployment started to fall, reaching 5 per cent by the end of the year.

In 1965 the tax cut was still expanding demand, but a passive fiscal policy would have resulted in a rising full employment surplus. Since the economy would not have reached the interim unemployment goal of 4 per cent with an increasingly deflationary fiscal policy, additional measures were designed to offset fiscal drag. A mid-year cut in excise taxes, Great Society expenditure programs, and an increase in Social Security benefits held the full employment surplus constant at $4 billion. Unemployment continued to fall to 4 per cent by the end of the year and output rose by 6 per cent.

In late 1965 two other factors started to affect the economy. Military spending on Vietnam began to accelerate and investment grew rapidly for the first time since 1956. Investment rose as a result of higher industrial operating rates, ample internal funds from the tax changes of 1962 and 1964, and general business confidence that the expansion would continue into the future. With investment spending rising by $2 or $3 billion per quarter, the economy quickly reached the interim unemployment target at the end of 1965.

Kennedy-Johnson expansion policies were successful in moving the economy to 4.0 per cent unemployment by late 1965, but the administration's stated goal had been to achieve the interim target by 1963. Until the 1964 tax cut, fiscal policies were simply not adequate to eliminate the gap between actual and potential GNP.

Policies to Restrain Demand

Achieving the interim unemployment target and expanding military and investment spending meant that fiscal policy had to be reappraised in late 1965. A new unemployment target had to be chosen, whether it be an absolute level or a rate of decline. If 3 per cent were the goal, policies needed to be even more expansionary. If 4 per cent were the goal, policies needed to move to a more deflationary position.

The new unemployment target had to be picked in an environment where prices had begun to rise at a faster pace. Increases in the Consumers Price Index accelerated from their accustomed level of 1 to 1.5 per cent to 2.5 to 3.5 per cent per year. Wholesale prices shifted from a position of stability to an increase of 3 to 3.5 per cent per year. The increases were small in comparison with other war situations and other developed countries, but they had accelerated. Part of the increase might have been due to nonrecurrent factors in food production and part to the speed of movement of the economy rather than to the level of unemployment. A portion might be eliminated by fiscal policies which reduced the expansion of investment, and part might be reduced by improvements in wage-price guideposts, but part of the increase was the necessary price for lower unemployment. It could only be eliminated by higher unemployment or by price and wage controls. The administration's fiscal policies moved to a slightly more deflationary position by increasing Social Security taxes $6 billion, by cancelling $1 billion in scheduled excise tax reductions, by reducing incomes $1.2 billion with a graduated withholding system for individuals, and by reducing corporate incomes $1 billion through cutting the time between corporate earnings and tax payments. Discretionary fiscal actions at the beginning of 1966 increased tax revenues by almost $9 billion, but large expenditure increases meant that the full employment surplus fell slightly from $4 billion to $3 billion in 1966.

Monetary rather than fiscal policies were the administration's primary weapon for restraining demand during 1966. The monetary fiscal policy mix was changed from one where fiscal policies were the primary instrument for *expanding* demand to one where monetary policies were the primary instrument for *restraining* demand. Whether the administration was following the proper mix depended on the nature of the unemployment target, the efficacy of monetary policy in restraining demand, and the desirability of large deflationary impacts on particular sectors, such as residential construction. The administration did not shift to the more effective fiscal restraints on demand since they did not think more restraint was necessary.

In addition to controlling the level of aggregate demand, fiscal policy also must be judged on how it distributes demand among broad sectors of the economy. Excess demand can exist in some sectors without existing in the entire economy. Regardless of aggregate unemployment goals, investment spending and the demands for military hardware by late 1965 and early 1966 were expanding demand in the capital goods industries faster than it could be met by existing capacity. If military procurement was necessary, private investment had to be cut, at least in the short run, until more resources could be moved into the area. In the

Fall of 1966 the administration asked for a suspension of the investment tax credit and the accelerated depreciation allowances for industrial construction to encourage reductions in investment spending plans.

By the end of 1966 administration policies produced an unemployment rate of 3.8 per cent and tolerated an increase in the Consumers Price Index of 3 per cent. The internal success or failure of these policies depends on whether the administration's goals were higher or lower.

FISCAL FLEXIBILITY

The success of the 1964 tax cut in moving the economy to higher levels of capacity utilization has probably significantly reduced public and congressional opposition to using tax reductions as a means of closing a gap between actual and potential output. Concerns about reducing taxes when the federal budget is in deficit have substantially decreased, even if they have not disappeared. The next time a tax reduction is requested congressional delays will probably be much shorter. Since conservatives have learned that tax reductions can provide a powerful counterweight to public expenditure increases they will probably become vigorous supporters instead of opponents.

Since giving money to voters is easier than taking it away from them, delays are apt to be much longer in situations which call for increased taxes. Here the temptation is to delay as long as possible or to use other policies to avoid unpleasant political repercussions. With this built-in asymmetric response, American fiscal policy will probably slip into the European mode where errors of excessive stimulation are much more frequent than errors of inadequate stimulation. In the postwar period, American errors were generally in the direction of inadequate stimulation. The situation is not apt to reappear.

An asymmetric ability to use fiscal policies will probably have some strong effects on expenditure policies. In recessions the conservative bias in favor of tax reductions and the speed with which tax reductions can operate to eliminate a gap between actual and potential output will create strong pressures to close any gap with tax reductions rather than with expenditure increases. Except for direct transfer payments, the preparation necessary to carry out effective expenditure programs means that they have a much slower effect on aggregate demand even when congressional approval is just as rapid. In boom periods when actual output is either above or attempting to rise above potential output, expenditure increases are unlikely since politicians do not like to reduce private spending in order to increase public civilian spending.

The situation most favorable to expenditure programs is one in which the economy is at full employment, but because of the fiscal drag the government needs to declare a fiscal dividend every year in order to stay at full employment. The fiscal dividend could easily be shared between tax reductions and expenditure increases. In the postwar period, however, there have been very few years that have fallen into this happy category. In the future, the probability of this situation occurring will not only depend on the end of the Vietnam war, but also on the government's ability to eliminate strong investment cycles. With investment cycles of the postwar magnitude, a positive or negative gap between actual and potential output will exist most of the time. Although fiscal policies are powerful tools there is little evidence that the political process is flexible enough to use them to bring the investment cycle under control.

NOTES

1. Thurow, L. C. and L. D. Taylor, "The Interaction Between the Actual and Potential Rates of Growth," *Review of Economics and Statistics,* XLVII (November, 1966), p. 354.
2. *Ibid.,* p. 357.

PART I

Diagnosing the Principles of Fiscal Policy for the Sixties

TOWARD FULL RECOVERY

Council of Economic Advisers

As established by the Employment Act of 1946, the Council of Economic Advisers advises the President on economic policies. The Council's Annual Report is the major place in which the President's fiscal policies are outlined and justified. In the first Annual Report of the Kennedy Administration in January, 1962, the CEA presented its fiscal policy goals and its analysis of why the economy had suffered from high unemployment for the previous five years. The Chairman in 1962 was Walter W. Heller; the members were Kermit Gordon and James Tobin.

THE OBJECTIVE OF MAXIMUM EMPLOYMENT

Reasons for Concern over Unemployment

The great depression led this nation, and most other nations of the free world, to assume national responsibility for the human tragedy and economic waste of involuntary unemployment. Unemployment had previously been regarded as almost solely the personal responsibility of the individual; now it came to be acknowledged as a charge on the conscience of the nation. The mass unemployment of the 1930's led to new understanding: that to be unemployed is not to be unemployable; that job opportunities for individual workers depend on national economic circumstances beyond their control.

There are three principal reasons why involuntary unemployment is a national concern:

From the *Economic Report of the President together with the Annual Report of the Council of Economic Advisers,* January 1962.

1. The human obligation to prevent and to relieve economic distress;
2. The basic principle of a free economy that an individual should be able to chose freely how to use his time, whether to work for pay or not; and
3. The economic waste of leaving productive resources idle.

Preventing economic distress

First, a wealthy nation cannot in good conscience permit its citizens to be inadequately nourished, clothed, or housed; its sick to be denied medical care; or its young to be deprived of schooling. Unemployment insurance and public assistance are recognitions of this social obligation. But they are not substitutes for the opportunity to earn income from useful employment. For the breadwinner and his family, unemployment means a reduction in living standards. Only about three-fifths of the unemployed in 1961 were receiving unemployment insurance benefits. Even those who were insured generally found weekly benefits a pale shadow of their lost wages. When the unemployment insurance program was inaugurated in the late 1930's, the goal was to provide benefits equal to about half of previous earnings.

Benefits now do not meet this standard. For all too many, unemployment has not been simply an uncomfortable interlude between jobs but a catastrophe of long duration; almost one-third of those unemployed in December, 1961, had been out of work for fifteen or more weeks and one-sixth had been unemployed for at least twenty-seven weeks. Family savings vanish when unemployment is prolonged.

Unemployment is not a perfect measure of the incidence of economic distress. Failure to find work does not entail poverty for some unemployed persons: women whose husbands have good jobs, young people who can fall back on well-to-do parents, older people who have assured livelihoods from property incomes or annuities, people who earn an adequate annual income from work at a seasonal occupation during part of a year. On the other hand, there are many causes of economic distress other than unemployment. Some persons, though employed, suffer from reduced and inadequate incomes resulting from failure to obtain more than part-time or occasional work, or to earn decent returns from long hours of self-employment on the farm on in the shop. Other individuals are not regarded as unemployed simply because, discouraged by a lack of suitable opportunities, they have abandoned the search for jobs. Included in this group are individuals with personal disabilities who can find jobs only when labor markets are tight.

Nevertheless, changes in unemployment are indicative of changes in the over-all magnitude of economic distress. The same conditions of general prosperity which lead to lower unemployment figures also lead to lower rates of involuntary part-time idleness, to better rewards from self-employment, and to more job opportunities for persons on the fringes of the labor force. While effective measures to provide adequate job opportunities will not solve all problems of economic distress, they will solve a substantial share of them. And without a successful policy against general unemployment, other attacks on poverty and insecurity stand little chance of success.

Assuring free choice

The second reason for national concern over unemployment is the basic principle of a free economy, embodied in the Employment Act, that "useful employment opportunities" be afforded "for those able, willing, and seeking to work." A free society abhors forced idleness as well as forced labor. This principle does not apply a means or needs test for job-seekers. It acknowledges that mature individuals should be able to choose for themselves how they spend their time, as between gainful employment, housework, leisure, and education. Involuntary unemployment can destroy morale and freedom of choice whether or not the individual is in economic need. Americans want to work. Neither welfare programs nor personal means can erase the frustration of the individual who is forced to conclude that society does not need or want his contribution. The general preference for gainful work over unemployment, however well compensated, is demonstrated by the low levels of unemployment in areas with buoyant labor markets, in occupations with ample job opportunities, and in the population at large during years of prosperity.

Avoiding economic waste

Finally, excessive unemployment is a waste of productive resources. When these resources are left idle, the useful goods and services they could have produced are forever lost to the nation. These losses would be enormously wasteful at any time. They are dangerous in a decade when the economy must not only meet compelling domestic needs but underwrite the defense of freedom throughout the world. In coupling maximum production and purchasing power with maximum employment, the Employment Act recognizes the losses of national output and real income associated with unemployment. An estimate of these losses in present circumstances is attempted below. Changes in the unemployment rate are roughly indicative of changes in the "gap" between realized and potential production. The same measures of policy which will lower unemployment will also raise national output closer to capacity to produce. The national economic losses associated with unemployment are, of course, quite independent of the individual circumstances of the unemployed. If housewives, elderly persons, and teen-agers on vacation from school are eager and able to produce useful goods and services, it is foolish and wasteful for the nation to forego their contributions.

Full Employment as the Objective of Stabilization Policy

The goal of the Employment Act is "maximum employment," or—to put it the other way around—minimum unemployment. Ideally, all persons able, willing, and seeking to work should be continuously employed. Involuntary unemployment is an individual and social evil. No one would prefer for its own sake a higher rate of unemployment to a lower one. But zero unemployment is unattainable. A more meaningful figure is needed to give content to the realistic and forceful declaration of policy in the Employment Act. A feasible interim goal must reflect a balancing of employment and production objectives with other considerations of national policy, within the limits set by the existing characteristics of the economy. Such a goal is set forth in the discussion which follows. We must not forget, however, that any practical unemployment goal is only a temporary compromise, and its attainment must never be an occasion for relaxation, but rather an incentive to search out ways to achieve a still lower rate.

The partial conflict which exists between minimum unemployment and certain other national objectives—and which imposes the necessity of striking a balance between them—results mainly from the fact that these other objectives are served by stability of the general price level. Given the existing structure of the economy and the nature of the processes by which prices and wages are determined, a serious attempt to push unemployment close to zero would produce a high rate of price inflation. The result would be a weakening of the competitive position of U.S. products in world markets, an arbitrary redistribution of real income and wealth, and a threat of even more serious consequences if expectations of further inflation should become dominant.

Happily, however, the conflict between the goals served by price stability and the goal of minimum unemployment is only partial. Stabilization policy—policy to influence the level of aggregate demand—can strike a balance between them which largely avoids the consequences of a failure in either direction. Furthermore, the degree of conflict can be diminished by private and public policies which improve the functioning of labor and product markets.

There are various possible causes of unemployment, on the one hand, and of inflationary pressure, on the other. These causes may be grouped into (1) those related to aggregate demand and (2) those related to the structure and functioning of markets. It is necessary to distinguish carefully between these two groups of causes in setting an appropriate target for stabilization policy.

The relation of aggregate demand and of structural causes to unemployment may be briefly described as follows:

(1) The total effective demand for goods and services—by consumers, businesses, and governments—may be insufficient to employ all the persons seeking work at existing wage rates.

(2) Workers may be idle while vacancies are unfilled. This may arise because the workers live too far away from the available jobs, are not qualified for them, or simply are unaware of their existence. In a dynamic economy, there will always be workers between jobs, some seeking new positions out of preference, some displaced by economic and technological change. New entrants to the labor force will similarly be unemployed while locating jobs suitable to their qualifications and preferences. The length of "frictional" unemployment for any one worker, and the size of the pool of frictionally unemployed, depend on how smoothly the labor market functions, how well the skills, experience, and qualifications of workers match the specifications of available jobs, how ready workers are to change residence and occupation, how adequate are facilities for training and retraining, and how rapidly displacements resulting from economic change are occurring. Structural unemployment may be regarded as an extreme form of frictional unemployment. It occurs when inability or failure to make the necessary adjustments concentrates unemployment of long duration on displaced workers in particular areas and occupations, while elsewhere jobs are seeking workers of quite different qualifications.

Similarly, aggregate demand and the structure of markets are related to the price level, as follows:

(1) Inflation may result from excessive aggregate demand. Demands for goods and services by consumers, businesses, and governments may add to a total which exceeds the amount that the economy can supply. Prices will be bid up in all markets, and, as business firms try to expand output in order to seize the profit opportunities presented, increases in wages and in costs of materials will follow. The resulting rise

in incomes will reinforce and renew the process. In less extreme circumstances, aggregate demand may press hard upon, but not exceed, the economy's productive capacity. Increases in prices and wages may occur nevertheless, reflecting the need to obtain additional output by using labor and capital more intensively—by making greater use of overtime labor, by attracting workers from great distances, by making employment attractive to persons formerly not in the labor force, and by making use of obsolescent capacity and inefficient production techniques.

(2) Upward pressure on prices may originate in those sectors of the economy where competitive forces are weak and large corporations and unions have a considerable degree of discretion in setting prices and wages. There are two ways in which wage and price decisions in these sectors may put upward pressure on the general price level. First, prices may be increased when demand is not strong in the aggregate or even in the specific industries involved. Because the prices of these industries affect costs elsewhere, increases in their prices tend to spread throughout the economy. Second, prices in these sectors may remain constant in the face of declining demand, although they rise in times of increasing demand. The result in the long run is an upward drift in prices in these industries, which again tends to be transmitted to the whole economy.

Expansion of aggregate demand is clearly the specific remedy for unemployment caused by a deficiency of aggregate demand. Excessive aggregate demand, however, is a source of inflationary pressure. Consequently, the target for stabilization policy is to eliminate the unemployment which results from inadequate aggregate demand without creating a demand-induced inflation. A situation in which this is achieved can appropriately be described as one of "full employment," in the sense that further expansion of expenditure for goods and services, and for labor to produce them, would be met by only minor increases in employment and output, and by major increases in prices and wages. Correspondingly, expansion of demand beyond full employment levels would involve a major sacrifice of the objectives served by price stability, and only a minor gain with respect to the goal of maximum employment.

The selection of a particular target for stabilization policy does not commit policy to an unchangeable definition of the rate of unemployment corresponding to full employment. Circumstances may alter the responsiveness of the unemployment rate and the price level to the volume of aggregate demand. Current experience must therefore be the guide.

In the existing economic circumstances, an unemployment rate of about 4 per cent is a reasonable and prudent full employment target for stabilization policy. If we move firmly to reduce the impact of structural unemployment, we will be able to move the unemployment target steadily from 4 per cent to successively lower rates.

The recent history of the U.S. economy contains no evidence that labor and commodity markets are in general excessively "tight" at 4 per cent unemployment. Neither does it suggest that stabilization policy alone could press unemployment significantly below 4 per cent without creating substantial upward pressure on prices.

When unemployment was about 5 per cent, as in 1959 before the steel strike and in the first half of 1960, the economy showed many independent symptoms of slack, notably the substantial under utilization of plant and equipment capacity. The wholesale price index fell at a rate of 0.2 per cent a year in the fifteen month April 1959-July 1960; and at the consumer level, prices of commodities other than food rose at a rate of only 0.6 per cent.

The economy last experienced 4 per cent unemployment in the period May 1955-August 1957, when the unemployment rate fluctuated between 3.9 per cent and 4.4 per cent (seasonally adjusted). During this period, prices and wages rose at a rate which impaired the competitiveness of some U.S. products in world markets. However, there is good reason to believe that upward pressures of this magnitude are not a permanent and systematic feature of our economy when it is operating in the neighborhood of 4 per cent unemployment. The 1955-57 boom was concentrated in durable manufactured goods—notably automobiles (in 1955), machinery and equipment, and primary metals. The uneven nature of the expansion undoubtedly accentuated the wage and price pressures of those years. The experience of 1955-57 is nevertheless sobering, and experience at higher levels of activity will be needed to indicate whether stabilization policy can now undertake a more ambitious assignment than 4 per cent unemployment.

There is no precise unemployment rate at which expansion of aggregate demand suddenly ceases to affect employment and begins to affect solely the general price level. The distinction between aggregate demand effects and structural effects is a matter of degree, both for employment and for the general price level. Sufficiently high levels of aggregate demand can, and have in the past, cut deeply into frictional and structural unemployment. When vacancies are numerous, the time required to find an attractive job is reduced. When there are vacancies everywhere, no one needs to travel far to find a job. And when no applicant for a job meets its exact specifications, the specifications may well be adjusted. Similarly, the degree of inflationary pressure arising from discretionary price and wage setting is not independent of the general strength of demand. Presumably, this pressure could be entirely eliminated by sufficient weakness in aggregate demand if that were the sole objective of stabilization policy.

But while stabilization policy would not be an ineffective cure for either one or the other of these economic ailments, it would be an extremely expensive cure. On the one hand, attempting to reduce frictional and structural unemployment by a highly inflationary expansion of demand would court disaster in our balance of payments position. On the other hand, an attempt to restrict aggregate demand so severely as to eliminate all risk of an increase in the general price level might well involve keeping the economy far below full employment. This would mean sacrifice rather than achievement of both of the major goals that price stability serves: Equity would be sacrificed because the economy as a whole, and the unemployed in particular, would suffer as a result of the manner in which a few individuals and groups exercise their economic power. Eventually, the balance of payments would also be weakened: under conditions of prolonged unemployment and excess capacity, the investment needed to keep our exports competitive in quality and cost would be unlikely to occur.

The 4 per cent interim goal refers to the global measure of unemployment as a percentage of the civilian labor force. An objective stated in terms of any of the other measures of unemployment discussed above would have the same implications for stabilization policy, for the various measures tell the same story with respect to the degree of over-all tightness in the economy. The particular numerical statement of the goal must, of course, change with the unemployment concept used. For example, 4 per cent in terms of the global measure is roughly equivalent to a rate of 2¼ per cent among married men living with their wives; the latter figure, though lower, is at least as serious as the former in its implications for the human consequences of unemployment. Corresponding figures for the other measures of unemployment are 4¼ per cent among experienced wage and salary workers, 6¼ per cent for the full-time equivalent concept, and, if the 4 per cent global rate is long sustained, a two-thirds of one per cent rate of long-term unemployment.

Unemployment of 4 per cent is a modest goal, but it must be emphasized that it is a goal which should be achievable by stabilization policy alone. Other policy measures will help to reduce the goal attainable in the future below the 4 per cent figure. Meanwhile, the policies of business and labor, no less than those of government, will in large measure determine whether the 4 per cent figure can be achieved and perhaps bettered in the current recovery, without unacceptable inflationary pressures.

Full Employment and Structural Unemployment

One way to raise the attainable level of full employment is to reduce frictional and structural unemployment by improving the mobility of labor and the efficiency of labor markets. The amount of frictional and structural unemployment varies from country to country and from time to time within any one country. It has sometimes been suggested that, though a 4 per cent unemployment rate was once achievable in the United States with adequate levels of demand, it is no longer a feasible goal because of increasing technological displacement of workers, rapid obsolescence of skills, intractable pockets of depression, and greater numbers of young people swelling the labor force. Careful analyses at the Council and elsewhere—notably in a recent report by the staff of the Joint Economic Committee of the Congress—lend no support to the view that frictional and structural unemployment is a rising proportion of the labor force. It would be wholly wrong, however, to conclude that improvement in the structure of the labor market is not both possible and of high importance.

The displacement of labor through changes in technology, consumer tastes, and the geographic distribution of industry is an inevitable part of the growth of a free and progressive economy. But the level of unemployment corresponding to any given pace of progress depends on the smoothness with which markets function. The size of the pool of unemployed workers, like the size of a pool of water, is determined jointly by the flow into it and the flow out of it. The flow into it depends on the rate at which workers leave jobs or are displaced and on the rate at which new workers enter the labor force without jobs. The flow out depends on the speed with which the unemployed can transfer to jobs vacated by retirement, and to other skills, other industries, and other areas where jobs are available in expanding sectors of the economy.

Economic policy can reduce the size of the pool by providing opportunities for vocational training and retraining, by improving the flow of information about job opportunities, by facilitating the relocation of displaced workers, by acting to reduce and eliminate discriminatory hiring practices, and by assisting in the rehabilitation of depressed areas through the renovation of public facilities and the attraction of viable industry.

The benefits to the United States from the pursuit of such policies are great. In their absence, many of our citizens become, in a real sense, victims of progress; they are condemned to prolonged periods of unemployment which benefit no one and inflict an unjust penalty on an arbitrarily selected few. In their absence, we can expect resistance to technological progress from those who would be harmed by it without prospect of reward.

The returns from such policies do not come instantaneously. For that reason, we should undertake them now, even while unemployment and excess capacity are widespread. There is still time to reap the benefits of the reduction of structural unemployment during the current recovery. But these policies are no substitute for an adequate level of demand. Experience tells us that the pull of expanding job opportunities is a vitally necessary condition for the success of policies to assure a better functioning labor market.

FULL PRODUCTION

Productive Potential

The Economic Report is required by the Employment Act to set forth "the levels of employment, production, and purchasing power obtaining in the United States and such levels needed to carry out the policy" of the Act. In accordance with the obligation to set forth the levels of production needed to carry out the objectives of the Act, the Council has made the following estimates:

1. In the first quarter of 1961, a gap of $51 billion (1961 prices, annual rate) existed between actual gross national product (GNP) and the output obtainable at full employment;
2. By the last quarter of the year, recovery had narrowed this gap to about $28 billion;
3. For 1961 as a whole, production averaged $40 billion below potential.

Estimates of this kind cannot, of course, be precise. But they are essential in order to specify, within reasonable margins of error, a current measure of "maximum production" linked to "maximum employment." They indicate clearly that this nation can achieve a huge bonus of output and income by making full use of its resources.

Higher output would have accompanied lower unemployment in the following manner:

(1) Actual unemployment in 1961 was 4.8 million persons. Given the

actual 1961 labor force of 71.6 million persons, two million of the unemployed would have been at work at an unemployment rate of 4 per cent.

(2) At full employment, the labor force would probably have been considerably higher in 1961 and production would have been correspondingly increased. Participation in the labor force is encouraged by greater availability of job opportunities. In recent years of slack activity, the actual labor force has been abnormally low relative to the number of persons of working age.

(3) Furthermore, a brisker pace of economic activity is accompanied by a higher average number of hours a week worked by those employed. Part-time jobs are converted into full-time employment, and overtime work increases in private nonfarm industry.

(4) Because of these three factors—less unemployment, larger labor force, and longer hours of work—labor input at full employment in 1961 would have exceeded actual labor input by more than 4½ per cent, the equivalent of seven billion man-hours. The added man-hours could have increased production by $24 billion, at existing rates of productivity.

(5) The higher productivity that accompanies fuller use of resources would have meant still more output. In recessions, business firms cannot cut back their labor force as fast as their output falls. Clerical help and sales and supervisory personnel are essentially "overhead." Moreover, while firms can and do lay off production workers, they do so only with reluctance, preferring both to maintain morale and to avoid the expense of hiring and training new labor when business activity recovers. Recessions thus produce on-the-job underemployment, which is reflected in depressed levels of productivity. In movements toward full employment, recession losses in productivity are regained. At full employment, productivity in 1961 would, according to past evidence, have been 2 to 4 per cent higher than it actually was. This gain is equivalent to a $10 to $20 billion increment of GNP. A middle estimate of $16 billion brings the total estimated gain from both sources to $40 billion.

These calculations receive further support from an alternative approach. Evidence on the relationship between output and unemployment suggests that actual GNP in mid-1955, when the unemployment rate was close to 4 per cent, was equal to potential output. The trend rate of growth of GNP, adjusted for changes in unemployment levels, has averaged about 3½ per cent in the post-Korean period. Thus the path of potential GNP can be represented by a 3½ per cent trend from actual GNP in mid-1955. The 1961 value of the trend exceeds actual output by $40 billion, which is equal to the sum of the components described above.

Plant and Equipment Capacity

Periods of slack and recession in economic activity lead to idle machines as well as idle men. Only once since 1949, at the trough of the 1958 recession, was there more excess plant and equipment capacity in U.S. industry than at the start of 1961. While increases in output during 1961 have led to fuller use of capital facilities, 1962 begins with considerable room for expanded output from existing plant and equipment, enough room to permit achievement of the full employment goal. This excess capacity is available to be tapped on demand. It is easier to expand employment at stable prices when tools are already available for new job-holders. Otherwise, capital might act as a bottleneck, obstructing the flow of increased demand for goods into improved employment opportunities for labor.

While unused capital is a reserve source of supply, it dampens the vigor of demand. Although much of investment is undertaken primarily for replacement and modernization, investment for expansion of capacity is important to aggregate demand as well as to economic growth. Inducements to expand plant and equipment are stronger when present facilities are fully utilized. The rate at which existing capacity is utilized also influences the ability of firms to finance investment out of retained earnings. Unused tools are a drag on profits. They yield no return and they impose overhead costs for maintenance and depreciation.

A number of significant points can be made:

(1) Measures of capital utilization, like unemployment rates, indicate the persistence of slack in the economy over the past five years. Even during the expansion of 1959-60, operating rates and the ratios of output to the stock of capital remained considerably below their 1955-56 level.

(2) Recessions are clearly marked by excess capacity in plant and equipment. Capital was most underutilized at the 1958 trough; the low point of early 1961 lies about midway between the 1958 rates and those of the 1954 recession. Because capacity grew slowly in 1958-61, excess capacity in early 1961 was smaller than in 1958 even though unemployment was just as large.

(3) Output gains must match the growth of plant and equipment capacity in order to maintain rates of capital utilization. Periods of slow advance in production, like 1956-57 and 1959-60, lead to declining rates of utilization.

(4) Considerable excess capacity remains in the economy despite the

rapid rise of utilization rates during 1961. While there is no clear benchmark of full utilization of capital, the operating rates attained in late 1955 can serve as a reasonable indication. If GNP had been at its estimated potential level in the last quarter of 1961, capital utilization rates would have been approximately at the levels attained in late 1955. Existing excess capacity in plant and equipment is thus compatible with full employment of the labor force.

ECONOMIC STABILIZATION

Insufficient demand means unemployment, idle capacity, and lost production. Excessive demand means inflation—general increases in prices and money incomes, bringing forth little or no gains in output and real income. The objective of stabilization policies is to minimize these deviations, i.e., to keep over-all demand in step with the basic production potential of the economy.

Stabilization does not mean a mere leveling off of peaks and troughs in production and employment. It does not mean trying to hold over-all demand for goods and services stable. It means minimizing deviations from a rising trend, not from an unchanging average. In a growing economy, demand must grow in order to maintain full employment of labor and full utilization of capacity at stable prices. The economy is not performing satisfactorily unless it is almost continuously setting new records of production, income, and employment. Indeed, unless production grows as fast as its potential, unemployment and idle capacity will also grow. And when the economy starts from a position well below potential, output must for a time grow even faster than potential to achieve full utilization.

The Postwar Record

Despite the recessions of recent years and the inflationary excesses of the early postwar years, the postwar record of economic stabilization is incomparably better than the prewar. The economy fluctuated violently in 1919-21 and operated disastrously far below potential from 1930 to 1942. The 1929 level of GNP, in constant prices, was not exceeded, except briefly in 1937, until 1939. The difference between the 17 per cent unemployment of 1939 and the 3 per cent rate ten years earlier is a dramatic measure of the growth of the labor force and productivity even during depression. Since the war, the economy's detours from the path of full employment growth have been shorter in both time and distance. There have been four recessions, but none of them has gotten out of hand, as did the decline of 1929-33. All of the declines have been reversed within thirteen months, before unemployment reached 8 per cent of the labor force. For this improved performance there are several reasons.

First, the war and preceding depression left business firms and households starved for goods. Further, wartime earnings coupled with scarcities of civilian goods, rationing, and price control, saturated business firms and consumers with liquid assets. For these legacies of depression and war, the economy paid a price in the inflations of 1946-48 and 1950, with delayed effects throughout the past decade.

Second, the structure of the economy was reformed after 1933 in ways which substantially increased its resistance to economic fluctuations. The manner in which government tax revenues and income maintenance programs serve as automatic or "built-in" economic stabilizers is described below. The New Deal strengthened and reformed the nation's banking and financial system with the help of new governmental credit institutions, deposit insurance, and loan and guarantee programs. These have virtually eliminated the possibility that economic declines will be aggravated by bank failures, foreclosures, and epidemic illiquidity.

Third, there is a significantly improved understanding of the manner in which government fiscal and monetary tools can be used to promote economic stability. Under the Employment Act and the climate of opinion which it symbolizes, the government has been expected to assume, and has assumed, greater responsibility for economic stabilization.

Finally, businessmen and consumers no longer regard prolonged and deep depression as a serious possibility. They generally expect recessions to end quickly; they anticipate a long-term upward trend in the economy; and they spend and invest accordingly. This stability of expectations is in part the result of stability achieved in fact, and reflects general understanding of the structural changes which have contributed to it. But expectations of stability are also a cause of stability—nothing succeeds like success.

Achieving Greater Stability

While our postwar performance is a great advance over that of prewar years, it is still far from satisfactory. We have had no great depression, but we have had four recessions. Even the relatively short and mild recessions of the postwar period have been costly. In the last decade, the nation has lost an estimated $175 billion of GNP (in 1961 prices) by operating the economy below potential. Industrial production has been below its previous peak nearly half the time since 1946.

There is general agreement that economic fluctuations in the United States are intensified by—if not always caused by—a rhythm in inventory investment, alternating between periods in which stocks are accumulating at an excessively high rate and periods in which they are being liquidated. But it is not beyond hope that stabilization measures, both automatic and discretionary, can be strengthened in force and improved in timing so as to compensate for inventory swings better than has been true in the past. If this is done the swings themselves will be dampened.

The possible gains from improved economic stabilization are impressive. Losses of production, employment, and consumption will be cut. More saving and investment will be realized, contributing steadily to the long-run growth of production potential. Business, consumer, and labor decisions will allocate resources more efficiently when they respond less to cyclical prospects and more to long-run developments. There will be less need and less justification for restrictive practices which are now designed to provide sheltered positions in markets periodically hit by recession.

It is true that an economy operating steadily at a high level of employment, with only limited excess plant capacity, is more subject to the risks of price increases than an economy with heavy unemployment and large unused capacity. However, the dampening of economic fluctuations may itself help to counter this tendency. Cyclical fluctuations have been exerting a "ratchet effect" on prices; costs and prices have been relatively inflexible downward in recessions but have been responsive to increases in demand during recoveries. Cyclical swings in total spending also tend to be accompanied by sharp and transitory shifts in the composition of spending. Because prices and costs respond more readily to upswings than to downswings, these rapid changes in the composition of demand impart an upward bias to the whole price level. These sources of upward price bias will tend to be reduced as a more even pace of advance is achieved.

To capitalize on the potential gains of stabilization requires skillful use of all economic policy, particularly budgetary and monetary policy.

THE FEDERAL BUDGET AND ECONOMIC STABILITY

Federal expenditures and taxes affect total employment and production by influencing the total volume of spending for goods and services.

Direct federal purchases of goods and services are themselves part of total demand for national output. In addition, the federal government makes "transfer payments" to individuals, for which no current services are rendered in return. Examples are social security and unemployment insurance benefits, and veterans compensation and pension benefits. Both purchases of goods and services and transfer payments add to private incomes and thereby stimulate consumption and investment. Federal taxes, on the other hand, reduce disposable personal and business incomes, and restrain private spending.

By increasing the flow of spending, additional federal outlays—with tax rates unchanged—have expansionary effects on the economy. Whether an expansion in spending—government or private—leads mainly to more output or mainly to higher prices depends on the degree of slack in the economy. Under conditions of widespread unemployment and excess capacity, businessmen respond to higher demand by increasing production; under conditions of full employment, prices rise instead. In the slack economy of 1961, for example, additional demand from both private and public sources was readily converted into increased production.

Built into the federal fiscal system are several automatic defenses against recession and inflation. Given the tax rates, tax revenues move up and down with economic activity, since most taxes are levied on private incomes or sales. Indeed, tax revenues change proportionally more than GNP. Furthermore, certain federal expenditures, such as unemployment compensation payments, are automatically affected by the state of the economy. Economic fluctuations, therefore, result in substantial changes in federal expenditures and revenues, even when basic expenditure programs and tax rates remain unchanged. With the present system of tax rates and unemployment compensation payments, a one-dollar reduction in GNP means a reduction in federal tax receipts and an increase in transfer payments totaling about thirty cents. Therefore, private incomes after federal taxes fall by only seventy cents for each reduction of one dollar in GNP. For this reason, any initial decline in spending and output is transmitted with diminished force to other sectors of the economy.

These automatic or built-in stabilizers moderate the severity of cyclical swings in the economy. If the forces causing a downturn in economic activity are weak and transient, the automatic stabilizers cushion the severity of the decline and give the basic recuperative powers in the private economy a better opportunity to produce a prompt and full recovery.

But if the forces causing the downturn are strong and persistent, the built-in stabilizers may not suffice to prevent a large and prolonged recession. Furthermore, they are blindly symmetrical in their effects. When economic activity quickens after a slump, the rise in federal revenues begins immediately and slows the recovery in employment and incomes. For these reasons, the task of economic stabilization cannot be left entirely to built-in stabilizers. Discretionary budget policy, e.g., changes in tax rates or expenditure programs, is indispensable— sometimes to reinforce, sometimes to offset, the effects of the stabilizers.

To be effective, discretionary budget policy should be flexible. In order to promote economic stability, the government should be able to change quickly tax rates or expenditure programs, and equally able to reverse its actions as circumstances change. Failure to arrest quickly a downturn in income, production, and employment may shake the faith of firms and households in prompt recovery and thereby lead to a cumulative decline. Delay in countering inflationary pressures may permit the development of a self-propelling speculative boom, with disruptive consequences to the domestic economy and the balance of payments. If moderate fiscal action can be taken quickly and can be speedily reversed when circumstances warrant, the dangers of over-stimulating or overrestricting the economy are much smaller than if fiscal responses are sluggish and difficult to reverse.

Fiscal policy can be made a more flexible and more powerful tool of economic stabilization by means that do not change the basic structure and level of taxation or the long-run size and composition of federal expenditure programs. Changes in the basic structure and level of taxation should be made by the Congress with full deliberation in the light of the many relevant considerations, including the long-run revenue needs of the government, equity among individuals and groups, and the effects of various taxes on economic efficiency and growth. Similarly, changes in the magnitude and content of government expenditures should represent the considered judgment of the people and the Congress on national priorities. For purposes of economic stabilization all that is needed of tax policy is temporary variation in the general level of tax rates within the existing structure, and all that is required of government outlays is timing of certain expenditures so that they bolster employment and purchasing power when the economy needs stimulus and taper off as it approaches full employment. In both cases, the form of action required for purposes of stabilization and the procedure for taking timely action can be agreed upon in advance.

BUDGET POLICY

The federal budget has influenced economic activity in recent years in two ways: through the workings of the built-in stabilizers, and through discretionary changes in the budget program. It is not easy to separate these two influences. In order to do so, it is necessary, first, to view federal fiscal transactions in the same accounting framework used to describe the whole economy. The national income accounts budget is a way of measuring and classifying federal transactions which accords with the national income and product accounts for the economy. Second, it is convenient to have a numerical measure of the expansionary or restrictive impact of a budget program on the economy. The full employment surplus is such a measure. This section discusses these two somewhat unfamiliar but highly useful tools and then applies them in an analysis of recent and prospective budget policies.

The National Income Accounts Budget

The effects of federal receipts and expenditures on the income stream are most accurately represented when the budget is viewed in the framework of the national income accounts. These accounts present a consistent record and classification of the major flows of output and income for the entire economy, including the transactions of the federal government. There are three major differences between the federal budget as it is conventionally presented (the so-called "administrative budget") and the accounts of the federal sector as they appear in the national income.

First, the national income accounts budget, like the consolidated cash budget, includes the transactions of the trust funds, which amount to about $31 billion per year and have a significant impact on the economy. Highway grants-in-aid, unemployment compensation payments, and social security benefits are examples of trust fund transactions. Because the traditional budget—or administrative budget—is primarily an instrument of management and control of those federal activities which operate through regular congressional appropriations, it excludes the trust funds, which have their own legal sources of revenue.

Second, transactions between government and business are, so far as possible, recorded in the national income accounts budget when liabilities are incurred rather than when cash changes hands. This adjustment in timing affects both government purchases and taxes, shifting them to the point in time at which they are likely to have their principal impact on private spending decisions. The choice of an accrual, rather than a cash, basis for timing is particularly important for the highly volatile corporate income tax. Since these taxes are normally paid more than six months after the liabilities are incurred, payments of corporate income taxes, as recorded in the administrative budget, run substantially below accruals in a period of rising economic activity. This difference is estimated at about $1.6 billion.

Finally, unlike the administrative budget, the national income accounts budget omits government transactions in financial assets and already existing assets. The largest omission is the volume of loans extended by the federal government. This volume is estimated at $2.5 billion net of repayments. While these loans have important effects on economic activity, they are properly viewed as an aspect, not of fiscal policy, but of monetary and credit policy, and are so discussed later in this chapter. Borrowers from the federal government, like borrowers from private financial institutions, acquire cash by incurring debts. They add thereby to their liquidity, but not directly to their incomes.

The Full Employment Surplus

As pointed out earlier the magnitude of the surplus or deficit in the budget depends both on the budget program and on the state of the economy. The budget program fixes both tax rates and expenditure programs. The revenues actually yielded by most taxes, and the actual expenditures under certain programs like unemployment compensation, vary automatically with economic activity. To interpret the economic significance of a given budget it is, therefore, essential to distinguish the *automatic* changes in revenues and expenditures from the *discretionary* changes which occur when the government varies tax rates or changes expenditure programs. The discussion that follows runs in terms of the national income accounts budget.

In Chart I this twofold aspect of fiscal policy is portrayed for the fiscal years 1960 and 1962. Since tax revenues and some expenditures depend on the level of economic activity, there is a whole range of possible surpluses and deficits associated with a given budget program. The particular surplus or deficit in fact realized will depend on the level of economic activity. On the horizontal scale, Chart I shows the ratio of actual GNP to the economy's potential, labeled the "utilization rate." On the vertical scale, the chart shows the federal budget surplus or deficit as a percentage of potential GNP.

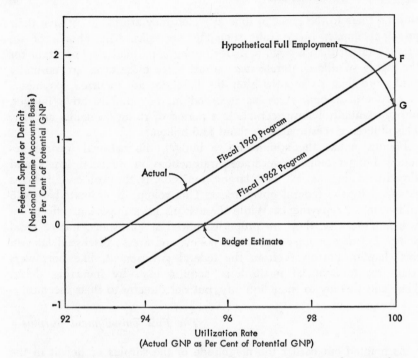

Chart I. *Effect of Level of Economic Activity on Federal Surplus or Deficit*

The line labeled "fiscal 1960 program" represents a calculation of the budget surplus or deficit which would have occurred at various levels of economic activity, given the federal expenditure programs and the tax rates of that year. For the reasons explained earlier, the same budget program may yield a high surplus at full employment and a low surplus or a deficit at low levels of economic activity. The actual budget position in fiscal year 1960, a surplus of $2.2 billion or 0.4 per cent of potential GNP, is shown at point *A*; this accompanied a level of GNP 5 per cent below potential. Had full employment been achieved that year, however, the same basic budget program would have yielded a surplus of about $10 billion, or nearly 2 per cent of gross national product (point *F* in the chart). The line labeled "1962 program" similarly shows the relationship between economic activity and the surplus or deficit, for the budget program of 1962; the expected deficit is shown at point *B*, and the full employment surplus at point *G*.

It is the height of the line in Chart I which reflects the basic budget program; the actual surplus or deficit depends both on the height of the program line and the level of economic activity. In other words, discretionary fiscal policy, by changing the level of government expenditures or tax rates shifts the whole program line up or down. The automatic stabilizing effects of a given budget program are reflected in the chart by movements along a given line, accompanying changes in economic activity. One convenient method of comparing alternative budget programs, which separates automatic from discretionary changes in surplus and deficits, is to calculate the surplus or deficit of each alternative program at a fixed level of economic activity. As a convention, this calculation is made on the assumption of full employment. In Chart I, the points *F* and *G* mark the full employment surplus in the budget programs of fiscal years 1960 and 1962, respectively. The statement, "the fiscal 1960 budget had a larger full employment surplus, as a fraction of potential GNP, than the 1962 budget" is a convenient shorthand summary of the fact that the 1962 budget line was below the 1960 line, yielding smaller surpluses or larger deficits at any comparable level of activity.

The full employment surplus rises through time if tax rates and expenditure programs remain unchanged. Because potential GNP grows, the volume of tax revenues yielded by a fully employed economy rises, when tax rates remain unchanged. Full employment revenues under existing tax laws are growing by about $6 billion a year. With unchanged discretionary expenditures, a budget line drawn on Chart I would shift upward each year by about 1 per cent of potential GNP.

The full employment surplus is a measure of the restrictive or expansionary impact of a budget program on over-all demand. Generally speaking, one budget program is more expansionary than another if it has a smaller full employment surplus. One budget program might have the smaller full employment surplus because it embodies greater Federal purchases of goods and services, in relation to potential GNP. By the same token, it leaves a smaller share of full employment output for private purchase. This means that full employment is easier to maintain under the budget program with the smaller surplus, because less private demand is required. It also means that inflation is more difficult to avoid, because there are fewer goods and services to meet private demand should it prove strong. Alternatively, one budget program might have a smaller full employment surplus than a second because it involves either lower tax rates or larger transfer payment programs. In that event, private after-tax incomes are larger at full employment for the first budget program than for the second. As a result, private demand would be stronger under the first program.

If the full employment surplus is too large, relative to the strength of private demand, economic activity falls short of potential. Correspondingly, the budget surplus actually realized falls short of the full employment surplus; indeed, a deficit may occur. If the full employment surplus is too small, total demand exceeds the capacity of economy and causes inflation.

But whether a given full employment surplus is too large or too small depends on other government policies, as well as on economic circumstances affecting the general strength of private demand. If the full employment surplus is too large, more expansionary monetary and credit policies may strengthen private demand sufficiently to permit full employment to be realized. Changes in tax structure, stimulating demand while leaving the yield of the tax system unchanged, might have the same effect. Similarly, restrictive changes in other government policies can offset the expansionary influence of a low full employment surplus.

THE NEW STAGNATION THEORY AND OUR CURRENT ECONOMIC POLICIES

Arthur F. Burns

Did the Kennedy Council of Economic Advisers determine the correct theoretical foundations for setting fiscal policy? Professor Burns argues that the Council mistakenly reverted to a stagnation theory of the American economy and that its calculations of the economy's potential rate of growth are questionable. He argues that an expansionary Federal budget is not necessary to reach full employment. Professor Burns is a former Chairman of the Council of Economic Advisers (1953-1956), President of the National Bureau of Economic Research, and a Professor of Economics at Columbia University.

In discussing so large a topic as our current economic policies, one must make a choice. I have decided to concentrate less on the policies themselves than on their theoretical foundations. Policies are always based on some theory. What I shall chiefly try to do, therefore, is to examine the economic theory that underlies the major economic policies of the new administration.

This task has been made relatively easy by the policy statement submitted by the Council of Economic Advisers to the Joint Economic Committee on March 6.

The Council's theory can perhaps be conveyed best by reading a few excerpts. According to the Council, "the American economy today is beset not only with a recession . . . but with persistent slack in production and employment, a slowdown in our rate of growth." Further, according to the Council, "economic recovery in 1961 is far more than a cyclical problem. It is also a problem of chronic slack in the economy —the growing gap between what we can produce and what we do

From "The New Stagnation Theory and Our Current Economic Policies," by Arthur F. Burns, *The Morgan Guaranty Survey* (May 1961). Reprinted by permission of *The Morgan Guaranty Survey* and Arthur F. Burns.

produce . . . Especially since 1955, the gap has shown a distressing upward trend."

The essential point of this theory is that, quite apart from the recession, there is increasing slack in our economy; there is a growing disparity between actual and potential output; in short, America faces a problem of secular stagnation.

The Council informs us that "the problem of unused potential becomes continually more urgent." The gap between actual and potential output has not only been growing, but has become very large. The gap is said to have been $32 billion for 1960 as a whole. Using annual rates, the gap is estimated at $40 billion for the fourth quarter of 1960 and at $50 billion for the first quarter of 1961.

But what, it may be asked, is the large and growing gap due to? The basic reason, we are told, is that there has been a retardation of investment. The rate of increase in the stock of capital per worker has been declining. The average age of our stock of equipment has been rising. And there has not only been a retardation of investment in business plant and equipment, but public investment has also been inadequate— that is, investment in education, health, research, and development of natural resources.

It follows from the Council's analysis that if our actual output is to approximate our potential output, investment in business plant and equipment will need to be substantially increased, and so also will public investment, especially investment in human beings.

Furthermore, if we proceed to increase both private and public investment sufficiently, our economic potential itself will rise more rapidly. According to the Council, the rate of advance that our economy now achieves when it operates at full employment is 3½ per cent per year. This rate will be higher if investment is carried out on a larger scale.

The theory that I have just sketched bears some resemblance to the Keynes-Hansen theory of secular stagnation, which dominated economic thought during the 1930's and 1940's.

Just as Hansen saw secular stagnation as he looked back in time, so the Council now sees the recent past. And just as Hansen saw secular stagnation as our fate in the future, unless appropriate remedial measures were taken in time, so the Council now sees the future.

Hansen, however, believed that private investment was bound to remain inadequate in view of the disappearance of the frontier, a declining rate of population growth, and a shift from capital-using to capital-saving innovations. Hence, he argued that it will be necessary to rely heavily on rising governmental expenditures if we are to escape a chronic condition of mass unemployment.

The Council is far less pessimistic about the prospects for private enterprise and investment. Not only does the Council argue that larger governmental spending can and will stimulate private investment, but the Council also proposes that some of our tax laws be revised in the interest of creating greater incentives for private investment. In other words, the Council seems to view the private economy as a dozing giant who, while not capable of realizing his potential through his own efforts, will come fully to life again and stay alive if the government does its part by spending more and by revising some of the tax laws.

Clearly, the Council's stagnation theory is gentler and less pessimistic than Hansen's. Indeed, it must be regarded as a gay and optimistic theory in the light of still older stagnation theories such as Friedrich Engels' or Thorstein Veblen's.

When Engels speculated about the future, he saw only the continuance of depression and the eventual breakdown of capitalism. And when Veblen turned to the future, he likewise saw chronic depression from which, to be sure, our people would be occasionally relieved but only through accidental developments.

The Council's diagnosis of the state of our economy, despite its stagnationist accent, has none of the morbid pessimism of earlier stagnation theories. A theory of secular stagnation such as the Council's therefore need not cause anxiety. Viewed coldly, it merely provides a warning. And the warning may be salutary if there is an empirical basis for the new theory. How substantial, then, is the evidence in its support? Let us turn to this question.

One piece of evidence cited by the Council is the progressive decline of business-cycle expansions in the postwar period. The expansion of 1949-53 lasted 45 months. The expansion of 1954-57 lasted 35 months. The expansion of 1958-60 lasted 25 months. In other words, successive upswings have been progressively shorter, and this is a symptom of noncyclical or secular slack.

In judging this evidence, it is necessary to recall that the expansion from 1949 to 1953 was dominated by the Korean War. This expansion might well have been shorter if the war had not lasted so long.

Historically, wartime expansions have always been exceptionally long. Indeed, the expansions of 1861-65, 1914-18, 1938-45, and 1949-53 are the longest business-cycle expansions that we have had.

Since the expansion of 1949-53 is clearly an abnormal case, it is best to put it aside. We are then left with the fact that the most recent business-cycle expansion was shorter than its immediate predecessor. There is nothing remarkable about this fact. Of itself it surely provides little reason to expect or to fear secular stagnation.

The Council cites, however, another piece of evidence—namely, unemployment was approximately 3 per cent at the peak of business in 1953, but about 4 per cent at the business-cycle peak in 1957, and about 5 per cent at the business-cycle peak in 1960. This evidence seems to suggest that successive upswings are becoming weaker.

However, as I've just noted, the peak in 1953 was a wartime peak of activity. We then had an overtime economy. It seems more sensible to regard the 3 per cent unemployment rate of 1953 as an exceptional case than to take it as a yardstick of economic performance.

This is as clear when we look back of 1953 as when we look forward, for the unemployment rate was about 4 per cent at the business-cycle peak of 1948 just as it was 4 per cent at the peak of 1957. Not only that, but the Council itself regards a 4 per cent unemployment rate as signifying a condition of practically full employment.

It is true that the unemployment rate was appreciably higher in 1960 than in 1957. This comparison is entirely valid. But one instance of higher unemployment of itself gives fragile support to the generalization that successive upswings are becoming weaker or to the theory that the gap between actual and potential output has a distressing upward trend.

The Council presents still a third piece of evidence. This takes the form of a direct measurement of the gap between actual and potential output.

Quarterly figures of the gross national product, adjusted for changes in the price level, are taken as a measure of actual output. Potential output is then measured by a curve which starts at the level of the actual output in mid-1955. This curve moves forward in time at an annual rate of increase of 3½ per cent, and it moves similarly back of 1955.

Why, it may be asked, does the curve depicting potential output start in the middle of 1955? The reason is that unemployment was then approximately 4 per cent of the labor force, and the Council regards a 4 per cent unemployment rate as a "reasonable target for full utilization of resources."

And why is this curve of potential output allowed to rise at an annual rate of 3½ per cent? Because, we are told, this rate "represents the rate of advance of gross national product (corrected for price changes) that our economy now achieves when it operates at reasonably full employment."

Once the curves of actual and potential output are drawn, the gap between them is obtained by subtraction. It is this gap which is said to show a distressing upward trend, especially since 1955.

The first and perhaps the most important question raised by this arithmetical exercise is why the curve of potential output is passed through the middle of 1955.

True, the unemployment rate was about 4 per cent in mid-1955 and actual output may therefore be taken as equal to potential output at that time. But the unemployment rate was about 4 per cent also in the second quarter of 1947, in the second quarter of 1957, and in other scattered quarters of the postwar period. Any one of these quarters or dates could have served just as well as mid-1955 for the starting point of the 3½ per cent curve of potential output.

The results, however, would have been very different. As the Council draws the 3½ per cent curve, the gap between actual and potential output in 1960 comes out $32 billion. But if the curve had been started in the second quarter of 1957, when we also had a full-employment output by the Council's criterion, the gap would have been only $20 billion.

And if the curve had been started in the second quarter of 1947, when we likewise had a full-employment output, the gap would have vanished. In fact, we would then have to say that actual output in 1960 exceeded potential output by more than $2 billion.

It is plain from these calculations that if we merely vary the starting point of the 3½ per cent curve, and do so without departing from the Council's logic, we can easily draw a more encouraging picture of the recent past than the Council has drawn.

Thus far I have followed the Council in assuming that our potential output has been growing at a 3½ per cent annual rate. I do not question the plausibility of this figure, but neither would I question the plausibility of a somewhat lower or a somewhat higher figure. We must reckon with the uncomfortable fact that small differences in the growth rate are capable of making a very large difference in projections of national output.

The Council has not described the precise derivation of its 3½ per cent growth rate. It seems clear, however, from what the Council does say that it did not use a method that is particularly appropriate on its own economic logic.

If it be assumed that a full-employment output exists when the unemployment rate is 4 per cent, then every figure of the gross national product at times when unemployment is at this level must express a full-employment output. A curve linking such figures will then automatically show the rate at which real output advances when our economy operates at reasonably full employment.

Unhappily, however, numerous pairs of such figures can be found in the postwar period, and some pairs yield a growth rate of less than 3½ per cent while others yield a higher rate.

Let me comment on one of the more decent calculations of this type. As previously noted, we had a 4 per cent unemployment rate in the second quarter of 1947 and again exactly ten years later. Between these two dates, our output grew at an average annual rate of 3.9 per cent— which is higher than the growth rate of potential output estimated by the Council.

Let us now see what happens when this 3.9 per cent curve is carried forward to 1960. At first blush, it might appear that the gap between actual and potential output would exceed the $32 billion figure computed by the Council. In fact, however, the gap turns out to be only $26 billion.

This illustrative calculation shows, once more, that it makes a good deal of difference whether the curve of potential output is started at one date or another. By starting the curve of potential output in the second quarter of 1957 instead of mid-1955, it is possible to convey, first, that the upward trend of the gap is smaller than the Council found, second, that the gap has lasted a shorter period, third, that all this is true despite the assumption of an appreciably higher growth rate of potential output than the Council estimated.

This concludes what I have to say about the Council's evidence in behalf of its theory. I hope that I have not left the impression that the new theory of secular stagnation is utterly without foundation. That would not be true. This theory *is* tied to some actual experience. But when the evidence is examined, it turns out to rest fundamentally on one fact, namely, that the business-cycle expansion of 1958-60 was exceptionally short and incomplete. When the expansion ended, our economy was still some distance from full employment.

I do not question the importance of this fact. Nor do I question its disturbing character. But I do question what inference can properly be drawn from this solitary fact.

I would urge two things. First, a theory which has such a slender foundation in experience must be viewed somewhat skeptically. Second, there is a better explanation of what happened between 1958 and 1960 than is offered by the neo-stagnation theory which of late has become quite fashionable.

Let us note, to begin with, that economic recovery proceeded very briskly until the spring of 1959. Between the first quarter of 1958 and the first quarter of 1959 the nation's physical output rose by 8 per cent. Between mid-1958 and April 1959 the rate of unemployment also fell sharply—from about 7½ to almost 5 per cent.

But soon thereafter a sharp retardation of economic growth set in. The expansion of business activity terminated in May 1960, having run its course in only two years and stopping at a time when the economy was still some distance from a full employment level.

Many factors undoubtedly contributed to the unsatisfactory character of the business-cycle expansion from 1958 to 1960, but I believe that three developments were decisive.

First of all, we had a violent shift in federal finances. Between the first quarter of 1959 and the third quarter of 1959 the federal cash deficit, allowing for seasonal factors, fell from an annual rate of $17 billion to $2 billion. By the second quarter of 1960, we were already operating with a surplus at an annual rate of $7 billion. Thus, in a period of little more than a year, we had a turnaround in federal finances of about $24 billion.

This was undoubtedly one of the very sharpest shifts of federal finance in our nation's history.

Second, the fiscal restraint on general economic expansion was accompanied—indeed preceded—by a tightening of credit conditions.

By mid-1959 commercial banks were already in debt at the Federal Reserve to the tune of $1 billion. The money supply stopped growing. Demand deposits diminished by nearly $4 billion between July 1959 and May 1960. Interest rates rose sharply, both on short-term and long-term loans. Indeed, long-term rates advanced faster than during a comparable stage of any business cycle during the past hundred years.

Still a third factor contributed significantly to the incompleteness of the expansion of 1958-60, namely, the protracted steel strike in the second half of 1959.

Anticipations of the strike first led to a sharp build-up of inventories and a boom psychology in the spring and early summer of 1959.

Once the strike came and continued to drag on, it caused both concern and confusion in the business community and led to some hesitation in placing orders for investment goods. The strike also led to some confusion in governmental circles and prevented early recognition, which otherwise might well have occurred, of the magnitude of the restraints that were being imposed by our government on economic expansion.

And when the strike finally ended, many business concerns—having in the meantime had an extraordinary stimulus and opportunity to re-examine their inventory policies—proceeded to practice new economies in managing their inventories.

In all these ways the steel strike contributed to an early end of the expansion which commenced in the spring of 1958.

If this sketch of the background of the recession is anywhere near the mark, we must attribute the incompleteness of the expansion of 1958-60 partly to the steel strike but even more to our governmental policies of restraint.

To be sure, these policies were designed to prevent further inflation and to restore confidence, both at home and abroad, in the management of our national finances. I have no doubt that these policies were sound and even essential. But, as happened in the event, they were pushed with excessive vigor and they were not checked in time.

On my reading of recent history, the neo-stagnationist theory which is now being widely used to explain the incompleteness of the expansion of 1958-60 is, therefore, quite unconvincing. To be sure, our economy faltered, so to speak, prematurely. But the early onset of recession was due to special factors, to factors of a kind that need not be repeated, rather than to some permanent or growing weakness of our economy.

I have dwelt on two very different interpretations of economic developments in recent years. These interpretations necessarily have different policy implications.

On the basis of the Council's interpretation, and to use its own language, "we face a stubborn problem of chronic slack, and the road to full recovery is a long one."

On the basis of my interpretation, there is no chronic slack of our economy. The problem of recovery that we face is not very different from that which we faced in 1949 or in 1954 or in 1958. Full employment is not a remote possibility. On the contrary, it may well be reached some fifteen or eighteen months from now.

In view of its interpretation of recent history, the Council logically concludes that "the expansionary effects of government programs will be welcome even if they occur well after the recession has been reversed."

I believe, on the other hand, that the mildness of the recent recession supports the thesis that the underlying forces of economic expansion are strong and that they have of late been only temporarily suppressed. I believe that signs of economic recovery are already here and are rapidly multiplying. In view of this fact and in view also of the substantial increases of federal spending that were initiated in the closing months of the Eisenhower administration and the further increases that have been set in motion by President Kennedy, I think that we would be courting inflation and a gold crisis if we now arranged new governmental spending programs so that they would mature when the economy is already advancing without them.

If we accept the Council's view that "we face a stubborn problem of chronic slack," the distinction between governmental spending to spur recovery and governmental spending to spur long-term growth becomes unimportant, and the same might be said of the distinction between governmental spending to promote social welfare and spending to promote economic growth.

On the other hand, if my diagnosis of the state of our economy is correct, these distinctions are vital. Thus, I would hold that improved medical care of the aged, however desirable it may be in the interests of human welfare, will do little or nothing to improve economic efficiency or to accelerate long-term growth, and that it is entirely misleading to favor better medical care of the aged, as is now being done, on the ground that it will also promote long-term growth.

Again, I would grant quickly that a liberalized social security program, such as President Kennedy advanced in his Economic Message to the Congress, would help to speed economic recovery. But I must go on and point out that the same can be said of any type of governmental deficit spending. Since the liberalization of the social security program is designed to be a permanent reform, rather than to serve merely as an anti-recession aid, I think that it is a mistake to advance such a program in the guise of a recovery measure. The Congress should pass this legislation only after full deliberation indicates that it is likely to promote the national welfare in the long run, and not merely in the months immediately ahead.

Once again, on the basis of the Council's analysis of the state of our economy, the problem of accelerating economic growth requires that we undertake greater public and private investment expenditures. I would readily grant this general proposition. However, the problem of accelerating long-term economic growth is excessively simplified when we suppose that it will be resolved merely by greater investment outlays.

Once aggregate spending is sufficient to maintain full employment, the rate of economic growth must depend principally on the rate at which economic efficiency increases.

Efficiency and productivity are undoubtedly promoted by some types of investment, but they can also often be promoted without any additional outlays or even with reduced outlays. We need think only of the restrictive practices that abound in construction work, in railroading, in agriculture, and in many of our manufacturing concerns.

I think that if we seriously want to accelerate economic growth, we will need to remove many of these impediments to efficiency, whether they arise from careless business management, or from the coercive power of trade unions, or from governmental legislation itself.

In the course of my remarks I have tried to indicate how a difference in interpretation of recent economic developments will lead to some differences with regard to economic policy. But I want to guard against any exaggeration of these differences.

Let me say at once that I see considerable merit in many of the proposals that the President has advanced for dealing with the recession.

I applaud his vigorous efforts to speed tax refunds, to enlarge the distribution of surplus foodstuffs to the needy, to speed early payment of dividends on veterans life insurance, to accelerate governmental lending under existing programs, to speed procurement which has already been scheduled, and to accelerate construction work which is already under way.

I admire the President's appeal for prompt enactment of a temporary program for extending the duration of unemployment insurance benefits. The Congress has already acted favorably on this request and I hope that the Congress will go further and enact, as the President has recommended, a permanent unemployment insurance law for coping with recessions.

I also feel encouraged by the new administration's recognition of the need to revise some of our tax laws in the interest of stimulating private enterprise and investment. I look forward hopefully to legislation along these lines.

But while I find the greater part of the President's recovery program entirely congenial, I am unable—as I have already stated—to regard liberalized social security programs, even though spending on them can get under way promptly, as sound measures for dealing with a recession.

I also doubt the wisdom of proposing a substantial increase of the minimum wage at a time of recession. I do not regard a lifting of the minimum wage as a useful anti-recession device, particularly at a time like the present when we are having a serious balance-of-payments problem.

Nor am I able to accept without some reservations the view that greater federal investment in education, health, housing, research, and resource development is desirable in the interest of accelerating the nation's long-term economic growth. I think that some of these types of expenditure may be justified on grounds of social welfare and that others may be justified on grounds of economic efficiency, but I fail to see how all of them can accelerate the nation's long-term economic growth merely because we now call them investment.

Nor am I able to accept the view that new and larger governmental spending programs on education, health, housing, research, and resource development should be welcomed even if they materialize well after the recession has been reversed. This particular view rests precisely on the stagnationist theorizing that I have taken some pains to scrutinize.

I have been forced by the nature of the topic on which you have invited me to speak to make some critical remarks on the economic thinking and policies of the new administration. But I also have found much to commend.

I deem it only proper to conclude by saying that the administration has avoided extreme economic views, that it has in no way shown hostility to business enterprise, and that the economic moves actually taken by the administration have been more prudent than some of its economic rhetoric has at times suggested.

THE COUNCIL'S VIEW

The Council of Economic Advisers

In its reply to Professor Burns' critique the CEA outlines what it considers the major points of agreement and disagreement, denies that it has a stagnationist position on the economy, defends its estimates of the gap between actual and potential GNP, and argues that an expansionary fiscal policy is necessary.

Economists are fond of saying (though tired of being told) that economics is not an exact science. It is thus not surprising that Professor Burns should differ on some important points from the conclusions reached by the present Council. We believe our analysis, based on careful research, to be sound and his criticism mistaken.

But if economics is not an exact science, neither is it guesswork. And so neither is it surprising that on some important issues Professor Burns comes to conclusions which parallel or coincide with the Council's views. We welcome the establishment of a broad area of agreement and hope that controversy can be focused where there are substantial differences of analysis and opinion.

A. MAJOR POINTS OF AGREEMENT

The four most important points of agreement seem to be these:

1. Professor Burns gives three mutually reinforcing explanations for the short and incomplete character of the 1958-60 recovery: the shock of the "violent shift" of the federal cash budget from deficit in 1959 to surplus in 1960; tightening of money and credit by the Federal Reserve authorities; and confusion in government and business circles and loss of momentum following upon the steel strike. With respect to

From "The Council's View" by the Council of Economic Advisers. Released to the press by Senator Paul H. Douglas, Vice Chairman of the Joint Economic Committee, on June 12, 1961, and printed in the Congressional Record on June 15, 1961.

governmental policies of restraint, he asserts that "they were pushed with excessive vigor and they were not checked in time." The Council has on various occasions mentioned the same points as reasons why the upswing after 1958 came to an end well short of full employment. These factors are not in dispute among the majority of economists.

2. Professor Burns apparently accepts the Council's position that it is weak aggregate demand, not an unyielding core of structural unemployment, that stands between us and a 4 per cent unemployment rate. This is implicit in his assertion that the American economy may well return to full employment in fifteen to eighteen months (from April). We do not neglect the problem of structural unemployment, but neither do we believe that the relatively high unemployment rate at the cyclical peak in May 1960 can be traced to special structural factors.

3. Professor Burns also applauds the Kennedy Administration for many of its programs for dealing with the recession and for its recognition of the need for revising the tax laws to stimulate private investment. Considerable agreement in prescription reflects considerable agreement in current diagnosis. The difference between Professor Burns and the Council in diagnosis concerns the probable speed of full cyclical recovery; the difference in prescription concerns the possibility of perverse timing of expansionary fiscal measures beyond those proposed before the date of his speech.

4. Even in his critique of the Council's analysis of the "gap" between actual and potential output, which occupies most of his attention, Professor Burns discloses large areas of agreement: he agrees that there *is* a gap, that "reasonable full employment" has been reached only fleetingly since 1956, that the peak from which the 1960-61 recession began was too low, and that the economy needs to do more than recover the ground lost in the recession. But here agreement ends, controversy begins, and labels are attached.

B. MAJOR POINTS OF DISAGREEMENT

1. "Neo-Stagnation" Theory

Unfortunately, Professor Burns has drawn attention away from issues and analysis by his emphasis on labels. This is doubly regrettable because the label he has chosen—"stagnation" or "neo-stagnation"—simply does not fit the Council's economic views. Having chosen this melancholy term to characterize the Council's position, he quickly distinguishes the Council's "stagnationism" from that of earlier economists by calling the

Council's version a "gay and optimistic theory." He also concedes that
the Council's theory "need not cause anxiety." What these disclaimers
reveal is (a) that a label is a poor substitute for analysis; and (b) that,
in this case, the label is wrong.

The distinguishing feature of the "secular stagnation" theory formu-
lated in the 1930's was pessimism about the prospects for high private
investment. Its exponents feared that full employment in a mature
economy was impossible unless private consumption and government
expenditure moved in to plug the hole left by severely declining investment opportunities. Rapid growth would be impossible under such
circumstances. The Council has expressed no such pessimism about
private investment or growth. Quite the contrary: far from suggesting
that more rapid growth is beyond our reach, we have shown that our
economic potential—the true measure of our capacity to satisfy needs—
has been growing throughout the postwar period at faster-than-historical
rates. In the light of slower growth in the last few years than in the
immediate postwar period, our contention has been that the growth of
our economic potential can be and should be accelerated. Our prescription for acceleration of growth has been consistent and clear: it calls
for a high-investment economy, a high-research economy, a high-educa-
tion economy.

2. The Gap: Facts and Estimates

Professor Burns criticizes the Council's "gap" analysis. The "gap" is
simply the difference between the actual output of the economy and
the output which could be achieved at reasonably full employment. The
existence of a gap at present is not in doubt. It is attested by the unemployment rate and by excess capacity throughout American industry.
The size of the gap cannot be measured with precision because the level
of potential full employment output cannot be directly observed. But
a reasonable estimate of potential output can be derived from careful
quantitative studies of the regularities of postwar economic life. Such
studies were the basis of the Council's gap figures. Without such figures,
it should be noted, the Council would not have the economic bench-
marks required to carry out the intent of the Employment Act of 1946.

The most detailed method used by the Council to estimate the 1960
gap is an analysis of the increase in output which would result from a
reduction in the unemployment rate to 4 per cent. Although this computation—carefully anchored in the actual experience of the U.S. economy
in recovering from the 1949, 1954, and 1958 recessions—is basic to the

Council's analysis, Professor Burns failed to mention it in his critique of our estimate of the gap.

The Council, together with many other economic analysts, takes a 4 per cent rate of unemployment as representing substantially full employment under present conditions. Given this conservative definition of full employment, the fourth-quarter 1960 unemployment rate of 6.4 per cent (seasonally adjusted) meant that excess unemployment amounted to 2.4 per cent of the labor force or 1.7 million workers. The Council's computation showed that a reduction of unemployment to the 4 per cent level would be accompanied by an increase of 8 per cent in output.

At first glance, it seems paradoxical that a reduction in the unemployment rate by 2.4 percentage points would yield a percentage expansion in output more than three times as large. The explanation is that full employment conditions have a number of favorable effects on output in addition to the basic one of putting the jobless back to work. First, new members are attracted into the labor force as job opportunities increase. Second, full employment brings an increase in average hours worked as part-time jobs are converted into full-time jobs and as overtime work increases. Third, a rapid increase in productivity per worker typically accompanies the fuller use of resources in an economic recovery; non-production workers, in particular, tend to be under-utilized in recession and their productivity rises as business picks up.

Another of the ways in which the Council estimated potential output, and reached an 8 per cent gap estimate for the fourth quarter of 1960, was by passing a trend line rising at 3.5 per cent per year through the actual output series at the middle of 1955. The annual growth rate of 3.5 per cent was selected after a study of trends in labor force and labor productivity. The middle of 1955 was chosen as a base partly because it represented a period of full employment but also—and this Professor Burns fails to note—because the results thus obtained were confirmed by independent gap estimates made by the Council and others.

Professor Burns points out that if other potential growth rates and other base points are chosen, they imply results for the 1960 gap which differ, sometimes substantially, from ours. The Council's confidence in its trend projection arises from the fact that it implies gaps which bear a close and reasonable relation to observed rates of unemployment in 1960 and previous years. To be plausible, alternative trends using different growth rates and different base periods should also have this important property of consistency. We have examined Professor Burns' suggestions in this light.

a. One suggestion was to use a 3.5 per cent trend of potential GNP anchored in the second quarter of 1957, when the unemployment rate was also near 4 per cent. We have compared the percentage gaps between potential and actual GNP implied by this trend with unemployment rates observed in every quarter beginning in 1953. To accept this potential trend one must also believe (1) that actual output was above potential throughout the years 1955 and 1956, during which time the unemployment rate fell to 3.9 per cent in only one month; (2) that the unemployment rate corresponding, on the average, to reasonable capacity output is 4.6 per cent.

b. Another suggestion was to start the 3.5 per cent trend in the second quarter of 1947. When the gaps implied by this procedure are compared with unemployment rates in the 1953-60 period the conclusions are: (1) that real GNP was above potential throughout the period from 1953 through 1957, and indeed that the recession of 1954 was a period of above-potential output; (2) that the unemployment rate corresponding, on the average, to reasonable capacity output is 6.0 per cent!

c. A third suggestion was to fit a trend rising at 3.9 per cent per year between actual GNP in the second quarter of 1947 and actual GNP in the second quarter of 1957. Continued to 1960, this trend yields a gap of $26 billion instead of our figure of $32 billion. It also implies: (1) that output was about potential from the very beginning of 1955 to mid-1957; (2) that the unemployment rate corresponding, on the average, to reasonable capacity output is 4.6 per cent.

As this evidence strongly confirms, the council's choice of a trend line for potential output was not capricious. We did not anchor it in 1947 or 1957, because to do so carries implausible implications about the performance of the economy in particular years and about the level of unemployment corresponding, on the average, to reasonable capacity output. And we did not use a higher growth rate than 3.5 per cent because of significant evidence that the rate of growth of potential in recent years has been lower than from 1947 to 1953.

We conclude from this review of the evidence that an 8 per cent figure for the gap in the fourth quarter of 1960 is grounded in persuasive evidence.

3. *The Gap: Explanation*

The Council does not hold the view that the gap is endemic to the American economy, or that it would not give way to standard fiscal and monetary measures to expand demand. On the contrary, we assigned responsibiltiy for the growth of unemployment and economic slack in recent years to "deficiencies in total demand," rather than to "changes in the structure of industry and manpower." ". . . [We] would not accept the idea that we have a chronic or growing long-run problem of unemployment that we can defeat by fairly standard fiscal and monetary means provided these are applied resolutely enough."

Professor Burns misread the Council's explanation of the gap when he said: "But what, it may be asked is the large and growing gap due to? The basic reason, we are told, is that there has been a retardation of investment." This misinterpretation is surprising in view of the pains the Council took to distinguish the problem of the gap from the problem of growth.

The gap problem is that demand has not been keeping up with the estimated 3.5 per cent annual increase in potential supply. The growth problem is that this 3.5 per cent annual increase falls short of an adequate rate of growth in our capacity to produce. We attributed the inadequate growth rate, not the growing gap, to "retardation of investment." It is faster growth, not the closing of the gap, that is the primary objective of increased private investment in plant and equipment and increased public investment in human beings. Undertaken in a time of economic slack, however, such increases have the welcome added virtue of helping to promote recovery by swelling the demand for goods and services.

A large part of President Kennedy's program for economic recovery consists of measures to expand consumption. For example, accelerated tax refunds and veterans' insurance dividends, temporary unemployment compensation payments, and aid to dependent children of the unemployed all expand consumer markets. These programs operate swiftly and surely to narrow the demand gap. Such measures as reduction of interest rates for small business, tax credits for investment, and expenditures for research, operate more slowly but have the virtue of simultaneously expanding demand and accelerating growth in productive potential.

4. Current Policy for Full Recovery

The major operational difference between Professor Burns' position and that of the Council concerns current policy—the degree and duration of desirable fiscal stimulus.

In his April 21 speech, Professor Burns stated that "we would be courting inflation and a gold crisis if we now arranged new governmental spending programs so that they would mature when the economy is already advancing without them."

Since April 21, in the course of the present recovery, President Kennedy has recommended to the Congress new or expanded programs in the fields of space, national defense, training and retraining of unemployed workers, foreign aid, and several others. These programs, if adopted, would increase federal expenditures in fiscal 1962 by $724 million. The Council must dissent from Professor Burns' implicit view that the enactment of such programs—all of them evoked by urgent national needs—will "court inflation and a gold crisis." On the contrary, we believe that there is room for such stimulation of the economy, and that public expenditures of high social utility ought not to be deterred by fears that the economy will soon be up against its capacity to produce.

Indeed, in our testimony we pointed out that the powerful federal tax structure would generate a considerable budget surplus at full employment, an issue which Professor Burns ignores. We agree with other witnesses before the Joint Economic Committee that this large latent surplus in the federal budget at present levels of expenditure makes full recovery more difficult. We have not stated, nor do we believe, however, that a federal surplus is incompatible with full employment. What we have stressed is the need for a rational allocation of the implicit surplus among increased government outlays, decreased taxes, and debt retirement to achieve higher levels of investment for growth consistent with full employment.

Professor Burns foresaw in April that "Full employment . . . may well be reached some fifteen or eighteen months from now," without any further special stimulus to the economy. According to the Council's estimates, full recovery in the third quarter of 1962 would require a 14.8 per cent increase in real GNP over the current quarter, and full recovery in the last quarter of 1962, a 15.8 per cent increase. Recovery has not proceeded at this pace in any comparable postwar period of expansion, except in 1950 under the stimulus of the Korean conflict. While it is not physically impossible for recovery to proceed that rapidly, current evidence suggests that it is highly improbable. If we were to equal the pace of recovery from the 1954 and 1958 recessions, the unemployment rate would exceed 5 per cent in the third quarter of 1962.

According to Professor Burns, "The problem of recovery that we face is not very different from that which we faced in 1949 or in 1954 or in 1958." The Council has not contended that there is any qualitative difference between the present recovery problem and earlier ones. Nor are the lessons learned from the errors of the past irrelevant to our present problem.

In every recession there is slack which must be taken up by expansion of demand; the important question is how much. According to our calculation, the percentage gap at the trough of the 1960-61 recession was greater than at the 1954 trough but about the same as at the 1958 trough. The Council has consistently stressed that the distance to full employment, not the drop from the previous peak, is the true measure of the magnitude of the recovery problem.

The 1958-59 recovery was accompanied by a much larger federal deficit than we will experience in 1961-62. In its initial year, it was also stimulated by a strong inventory buildup in anticipation of the steel strike. As Professor Burns himself shows, a sharp reversal of the federal fiscal position contributed to the premature end of the recovery. In retrospect, expenditure programs begun in 1958-59 and continuing or maturing in 1960 would not have been poorly timed. On the contrary, they would have given the economy a sustained stimulus just when the inevitably temporary stimulus of rapid inventory buildup was exhausted.

The Council believes that all governmental programs must meet the severe test of social priority relative to other public and private uses of the nation's economic resources. This is true of government spending to promote long-term economic growth, and of government outlays for social welfare. We would not support for purposes of recovery any programs which cannot meet this test. But a time of economic slack may be an opportune occasion for initiating programs of high national priority which have been waiting for room in the government budget and in the economy. The budget must not, of course, be built up by irreversible commitments during recessions to a level which would be regarded as undesirable at full employment. But some programs are reversible. Moreover, the needs of the nation, the growing "latent surplus" produced by the revenue system, and the general growth of the economy indicate that there is economic room for the increases in federal expenditure recommended by the President since April.

The Council is not in any sense proposing that the monetary and fiscal brakes be removed from our economic machine. If the recovery moves more rapidly than we now expect, these brakes can be applied to avert inflationary hazards. But the very existence of brakes permits the machine to go faster with safety. In a year of urgent needs and great opportunities there is little reason to lose precious time, production, and employment.

GROWTH ECONOMICS: THE CRUCIAL ISSUES

Leon H. Keyserling

Leon H. Keyserling, former Chairman of the Council of Economic Advisers (1949-1953), consulting economist and attorney, and President of the Conference on Economic Progress criticizes the Council of Economic Advisers for not providing a consistent frame of reference for their policies and for the inadequacy of their recommendations. He argues that extra stimulus for investment is not needed and that the CEA has substantially underestimated the potential rate of growth. The low potential growth leads to excessively timid fiscal policy proposals.

ESSENTIAL TOOLS

The minimum requirements for analysis that will serve as a guide to nation-wide economic policies are two. First, there needs to be constructed a detailed portrayal of the economy in action for a substantial number of years past. This portrayal, which has sometimes been called a "nation's economic budget," but which I have suggested calling an "American economic performance budget," should depict the main developments in production and employment, and define for purposes of critical evaluation how far these actual developments fell short of desirable and feasible objectives (both quantitatively and qualitatively in terms of priorities of private and public needs).

The performance budget should also analyze the various main flows of income and spending, as affected by market forces and by major private and public economic policies, and discern how these flows deviated from the requirements for optimum economic performance. And finally, the performance budget should delineate, subject to human fallibility, what alternative private and public economic policies, in their

From "Growth Economics: The Crucial Issues," *Business Horizons* (Winter 1961). Reprinted by permission of *Business Horizons* and Leon H. Keyserling.

impact upon income flows and other motivating economic forces, would have brought actual performance closer to the optimum.

On the basis of this analysis of the past and other relevant factors, there should also be constructed an economic performance budget for a number of years ahead, embodying the same essential components. This should be used as a rigorous guide to important public policies at the federal level, and as a consensual or voluntary guideline to private economic policies of nation-wide significance.

Neither the Council of Economic Advisers nor the President has thus far revealed such a performance budget to the public. I believe a budget of this kind essential if the Congress and the people are to understand our situation. Further, it would appear that the council so far has not been guided by the development of such a performance budget even within its inner offices. Only the lack of such a budget explains how the very able members of the council could have developed (in the judgment of many excellent economists) programs and policies so far short of what is required for the tasks at hand.

Aside from the quantitative insufficiency of the programs and policies set forth, the absence of a performance budget means that in large measure these programs and policies have had no common frame of reference, have not been adequately tested for consistency, and in part have been misdirected. To spell out these assertions, I need to indicate some of my own findings.

POOR PERFORMANCE TO DATE

Basically, I believe that our poor economic performance since the end of the Korean conflict has been due to the failure of effective aggregate demand to keep up with and make use of the *actual* growth in the labor force and productivity. This explains the long and increasing departure from maximum employment and production. It is also true that the actual growth in the labor force, and especially in productivity, would have been considerably higher if the large and growing economic slack caused by the inadequacy of aggregate demand had not seriously repressed the growth rate in both of these factors.

It follows from this analysis that we would have needed very specialized measures to improve the quality and structure of the labor force and to accelerate productivity growth (such as some specialized incentives to investors) if we had wanted to maintain an average annual GNP growth rate anywhere approximating the World War II annual average rate of about 9 per cent merely through the impact of an adequate level of aggregate demand upon utilization and growth in the labor force and productivity.

For the period 1953-60 as a whole measured at actual price levels, there were deficiencies in public outlays, occurring almost entirely at the federal level, as the states and localities strained their resources to advance as fast as they could. There were deficiencies in private consumer outlays, resulting in part from unsatisfactory income distribution affecting the relative propensity to spend and to save, but resulting more importantly from deficiencies in consumer incomes. These deficiencies included the gross deflation of farm income, the inadequate advance of both total wages and wage rates in the overall, and the miserable reluctance to expand sufficiently such consumer-oriented public programs as old age insurance and pensions, welfare spending, and minimum wage protection.

The deficiency in private business investment, which occurred for the period as a whole but not throughout the period, was not occasioned by harshness in the tax laws, nor by inadequate levels of profits and funds and other incentives during the boom periods. Rather, this deficiency reflected the sharp cutbacks in profits and incentives and business investment that occurred when the booms were followed by stagnation and recession, because of the insufficient demand for ultimate products on the part of consumers and governments. During the boom periods, indeed, the relationship between prices and wages in the key industries resulted in relative trends of profits and wages that yielded increasing profit margins per unit of sales and nonsustainably high rates on investment in plant and equipment.

As a result, these got further and further out of line with effective increases in real wages and other sources of ultimate buying strength. For example, during the period 1954-56, investment in plant and equipment grew about eight times as fast as ultimate private and public demand, and grew about five times as fast during the period 1958-60. This analysis serves also to indicate the nature of the "new inflation" when it occurred, and the fallacy of attributing it to wage rate increases that allegedly necessitated price increases. In addition to the inadequate level of federal outlays, the tax policy and the monetary policy imposed excessive restraints upon the over-all economy, and were much too regressive in terms of their relative impacts upon investment and consumption.

To quantify this analysis, the 2.5 per cent annual rate of economic growth for 1953-60 meant a loss of about 18.5 man-years of employment opportunity, and a production loss of more than $260 billion, measured in uniform 1959 dollars. The deficiency in private consumer expenditures was about $170 billion, in public outlays for goods and services at all levels about $30 billion, and in gross private investment including net foreign more than $60 billion. A substantial part of this investment deficiency, however, was in residential construction rather than in investment in expanding the means of production.

FUTURE POLICIES AND GOALS

Even though we now happen to be in another boom period—albeit a seemingly weaker boom than preceding ones—I have already indicated that I see very little fundamental difference between our basic situation now and in earlier periods since 1953.

Consequently, our long-range economic policies, geared to an economic performance budget that is reasonably attuned to our growth potentials and that carefully analyzes the sources of our recent and current difficulties, should move along these lines: a much larger expansion of federal outlays, directed toward domestic programs so far as not needed for immediate international purposes; great expansion of the public programs, such as social security, that increase consumer incomes by means other than direct federal spending; development of guideline studies pointed toward formulas for wage rate increases that, consistently with a stable price level, will help wages to exert their appropriate role in the expansion of total consumption; and vigorous measures to lift farm income through adjustment of supply and expansion of demand both at home and overseas. For reasons already stated, I believe that such efforts would induce an entirely adequate level of business investment, and indeed, the real problem would again be to prevent this investment from becoming too ebullient.

Such a combination of policies would balance the federal budget or even yield a surplus in those years when we were close enough to full resource use to justify such tight budget policies. Actually, current tax rates are in the main too high for this purpose because they would yield a surplus far short of full resource use, and there should be some tax reductions favorable to low-income and middle-income consumers. There should also be considerably more liberalization of monetary policy, with lower long-term and short-term interest rates.

I shall now quantify these objectives in order to indicate their implications, restricting myself here to the goals for 1962. I developed these early in 1961, consistent with long-range goals through 1965. While it now seems almost impossible that these goals could be attained in 1962 because of neglect, they are nonetheless indicative of the nature of the tasks ahead. Compared with fourth quarter, 1960 (annual rates seasonally adjusted), total national production should be up $86 billion; net farm income up $6 billion; transfer payments up $8 billion; gross private investment up $23 billion; residential nonfarm construction up $8 billion; and public outlays for goods and services up almost $14 billion at the federal level, and more than $4 billion at the state and local level.

CURRENT INADEQUACIES

Inadequacies in Policies

It is discouragingly obvious that little of the official programmatic thinking is in line with this analysis or adjusted to these goals. I feel this way not only about the short-range economic outlook (which I have already discussed in citing the employment and production trends thus far) but also about the long-range outlook. Even if the Congress were to respond favorably and quickly to all that the administration has so far proposed, including the logical expansion in future years indicated or implied, I question seriously whether our average annual growth rate during the five-year period 1961-65 would be appreciably higher than the dismally inadequate rate during 1953-60.

Errors in Tax Approaches

A significant example of faulty analysis is the proposal for special tax concessions to investors made by the President earlier this year with the public support of the Council of Economic Advisers. While this proposal was not adopted, it is generally believed that the Secretary of the Treasury and others are developing an even broader range of tax concessions for presentation next year. In recent weeks, in fact, the Treasury has granted some tax concessions to encourage investment in plant and equipment.

The main reasons advanced by the Council of Economic Advisers for this kind of tax thinking is that a GNP growth rate much above 3.5 per cent annually, after full recovery is achieved, depends upon an annual productivity growth rate much higher than 2.0 per cent (assuming a growth rate in the labor force of about 1.5 per cent); that this higher growth rate in productivity requires a much higher ratio of business investment to GNP than has pertained in recent years; and that this in turn requires special tax concessions.

Let us put aside the point that we need to achieve full economic restoration before we start sustaining it, and that stimulating investment relative to private and public demand for ultimate products would seem foolish until after full recovery. But even thereafter, granted that the average annual growth rate both in productivity and in the investment that affects it have *averaged* much too low since 1953 as a whole, the reasons for the low growth rate in investment have been entirely different from those that might call for tax concessions. And the reasons for the low productivity growth rate average have been only in part technological; to a large extent, they have been due to economic slack— a fact that the advisers admit. In addition, the advisers have adduced no arguments in support of their claim that the ratio of investment to GNP should be higher for the long pull than in recent years, except reasoning by analogy to the years immediately following World War II, which involved entirely different problems. Furthermore, there is no indication that an adequate level of ultimate demand has not induced an adequate ratio of investment to GNP—in the past, the ratio when ultimate demand was high has tended to get too high and to get us into trouble.

In any event, measures to provide special incentives to investors should be accompanied by compatible measures to help expand other sectors in order to provide equilibrium. The idea that high investment is automatically sustainable is negated by all experience. But without a performance budget, the tax ideas of the advisers have been developed in a void, and have no contact with reality.

There is other evidence that the economic advisers do not yet have the comprehensive view of the economy and the integrated approach to policies that a performance budget would provide. In their testimony before the Joint Economic Committee on March 6, 1961, the advisers stated that the personal saving ratio during the last half of 1960 was "abnormally high." To a question posed by a member of the committee, the advisers subsequently replied:

Strength in consumer spending would be a welcome stimulus to our economy, which is suffering from inadequate demand. But a low saving ratio is not a *sine qua non* of recovery if investment or public expenditure expands sufficiently. The higher the personal saving ratio, the more the burden in restoring and maintaining full employment falls on investment demand. If investment demand is to expand sufficiently, both the tax system and the monetary policy must provide adequate incentives to investment. There are advantages to a sustained prosperity of this kind.

This seems to me an extremely superficial statement. It reflects a common error of the economic model makers who stop short of the real problem, namely, the error of assuming that a level of GNP high enough to sustain full prosperity can result merely from playing around with the figures representing the components of GNP until these figures add up to the desirable GNP.

The error begs the whole question of a sustainable relationship between the expansion of productive capacities and the expansion of demand for ultimate products. This is the essential problem in the American economy. It is a problem that the advisers, in their public analysis and policy discussions to date, have hardly touched. If they came to grips with this problem, they would change many of their ideas, including their ideas concerning taxes. They might find, for example, that the propensity of consumers to spend might be encouraged if tax changes were directed toward improving the distribution of personal income after taxes, and that these types of changes would, on grounds of both equilibrium and equity, be far safer and sounder than using tax concessions to stimulate some more nonsustainable investment booms.

The Faulty 3.5 Per Cent Growth Rate

The tax mistake proceeds from the economic advisers' faulty conclusion that a 3.5 per cent GNP growth rate is "normal" and consistent with sustained full employment after it is achieved. This conclusion, since it is based upon the idea that a 2.0 per cent average annual increase in productivity is normal, leads naturally to the idea that a 2.0 per cent nation-wide average increase in wage rates would be about correct. It also leads to the conclusion that, in order to get a higher GNP growth rate, tax policies must be used as the advisers suggest.

However, the 3.5 per cent figure, for the purposes used by the advisers, would not seem to bear close scrutiny. To be sure, during the four decades 1922-60 (1922 being an appropriate base year after World War I), the average annual rate of growth in total national production was 3.4 per cent, measured in uniform 1959 dollars. And if we exclude the Great Depression and the far from satisfactory recovery during the period 1929-39, the World War II and reconversion years 1939-47, and the Korean conflict years 1950-52, the average annual rate of growth since 1922 was about 3.7 per cent.

But this 3.7 per cent figure is a very long-term average performance that spans good and bad years. It includes the years 1953-60, when the average annual growth rate of only 2.5 per cent carried us further and further away from maximum employment and production. The growth rate was more than 4.5 per cent during the peacetime prosperity period 1922-29, which was not characterized by excessive pressure upon productive resources or by an "undesirably low level of unemployment. During the predominantly peacetime period 1947-50, the annual average was about 4.0 per cent, despite a somewhat high average level of unemployment and one substantial recession. And during the period 1947-53, divided somewhat equally between peacetime and limited war and therefore roughly comparable as a whole to the period since 1953, the annual average growth rate was 4.8 per cent, despite average employment considerably below maximum.

In view of this record, my estimate—that an average annual growth rate of about 4.2 per cent during the period 1953-70 would have been consistent with sustained maximum utilization of our growing productive resources—is perhaps conservative. Indeed, if we go all the way back to 1922, no period of significant length can be found in which a lower growth rate resulted in anything approximating maximum employment and production. In view of the productivity trends discussed below, I estimate that an average annual growth rate of about 5.0 per cent, or only very slightly higher than the 4.8 per cent rate during the period 1947-53, would be the optimum for the years immediately ahead, once maximum employment and production are restored. To return to full prosperity by the end of 1962, an average annual growth rate of about 8.0 per cent would be required in 1960-62. We are not likely to achieve it.

Vulnerable Productivity Analysis

Nor is there much support in the data for the economic advisers' idea that it is reasonable to expect only a 2.0 per cent average annual growth rate in productivity under conditions of fairly full resource use. The average annual growth in productivity for the entire private economy is estimated at 0.5 per cent during the period 1910-20; it accelerated to 2.4 per cent during the period 1920-30; and it accelerated further to 2.6 per cent during the period 1930-40. During the most recent of these three decades, the continued advance in technology more than counteracted the adverse effect upon productivity of depression levels of unemployment. Indeed, it may be that the brutal disemployment of workers during the Great Depression sacrificed nation-wide efficiency to per-unit "efficiency." The period 1940-50 showed an average annual productivity growth rate at the still faster rate of 3.0 per cent, with a higher rate in the post-World War II period.

As a whole, the most recent ten years have shown a serious decline in the rate of productivity growth. But this adverse trend did not start at the beginning of the decade. During the period of reasonably full employment, 1947-53, the average annual rate of productivity growth had accelerated still further to 4.1 per cent. And even during the period 1950-55, in which conditions of moderate economic slack prevailed, the productivity growth rate averaged 3.8 per cent, or much higher than the 1940-50 average. But during the 1953-60 period, a period of relatively large economic slack, the productivity growth rate averaged only 2.6 per cent; and during the 1955-60 period, a period of still greater economic slack, the productivity growth rate fell to an average of only 2.1 per cent.

Since, broadly speaking, progress in science, technology, and automation has continued to accelerate, this disturbing decline in the productivity growth rate has not been due primarily to deficiencies in technological capabilities. Instead, it has represented considerable inefficiency in the use of man power and existing plant and equipment, brought about by large and growing economic slack. Moreover, under the incentives of higher ultimate demand, our technological capabilities *in being* would have increased through investment much more rapidly than they actually did.

The President's economic advisers stress the fact that productivity gains are adversely affected by economic slack, and that productivity speeds up greatly as the economy moves closer to full operation. Indeed, the advisers point out that, during periods when unused capacities are being sharply reduced, the average annual productivity gains tend to be about 3.3 per cent. There is no reason to assume that these gains would be lower at reasonable full utilization of capacities; in fact, they might well be higher.

Department of Labor studies and statements by the Commissioner of Labor Statistics reinforce the proposition that there has been a distinct acceleration in the rate of productivity gains in the private economy during the past five decades. The relevant productivity figures derived by the Bureau of Labor Statistics indicate an annual productivity gain potential ranging between 3.5 and 3.9 per cent under conditions of high capacity utilization.

These results are all consistent with the proposition that an average annual GNP growth rate of about 5.0 per cent would result in the years shortly ahead if reasonably full utilization of resources were maintained. The main policy measures put forward by the economic advisers to lift the growth rate above 3.5 per cent do not, however, correctly size up the elements in the problem; indeed, these policies would work against rather than in favor of equilibrium at full prosperity.

Policy Deterioration

In recent months and weeks, there have been no indications that the government is improving its thinking or sharpening its tools in order to achieve more rapid economic recovery or more adequate growth.

For example, at the technical level, we hear more and more to the effect that programs which might well serve these purposes must be held in check in view of our international balance of payments problem. As the general economic policies of the administration move closer and closer to those of the previous administration, the balance of payments problem—real though it is—is being used in a scare campaign to turn us away from much of what we need to do. Similarly, the real aspects of the inflationary problem were pumped up into a scare during the Eisenhower administration for the same purpose.

If the economic advisers used an economic performance budget to integrate a thorough analysis of our international economic problems with our domestic economic problems, they would soon discover that a sustained and adequate rate of economic growth in the United States would do more than all else to reduce the real or alleged overseas competitive threat to our well-being, not to speak of improving overseas confidence in the American economy and therefore the American dollar. In addition, the advisers ought to be helping the President to tell the country that new instrumentalities can be devised to reduce our slavish dependence upon gold, and to maximize the real wealth and prospects that we are now sacrificing by our reliance on outmoded shibboleths. Unfortunately, the advisers seem most recently to be abetting rather than resisting the faulty use of the balance of payments problem.

The economic advisers may also be taken to task for joining in, instead of continuing to resist, the rosy optimism now pervading the administration on the economic front. When high technicians in even the Department of Labor put in their press releases no better explanation of the failure to reduce unemployment in September than hurricane "Carla," when Cabinet officers and economic advisers are talking about a recovery that has "exceeded our highest predictions," and when some of them who should know better are saying that the only remaining unemployment problem is "hard core" or "structural," I shudder to think of our economic future in the face of world events.

PART II

A Program to Reach Full Employment

STIMULATING INVESTMENT

Douglas Dillon

The fiscal strategy of the Kennedy Administration in 1961 and 1962 was to increase aggregate demand by stimulating investment. American growth rates had been lagging behind our Russian competitors and President Kennedy had made a reduction in the gap one of his major campaign issues. If a large increase in investment could have been induced, it would have both raised America's potential rate of growth and started the economy moving toward full employment. Douglas Dillon outlines the Administration's investment tax credit and depreciation proposals designed to stimulate investment and stresses the role of investment in promoting growth. Mr. Dillon was Secretary of the Treasury at the time.

American industry must compete in a world of diminishing trade barriers, in which the advantages of a vast market, so long enjoyed here in the United States, are now being or are about to be realized by many of our foreign competitors. Our balance-of-payments position, as well as our standard of living in the long run, can be improved or even maintained only if we can increase our efficiency and productivity at a rate at least equal to that of other leading industrialized nations. These nations have now largely achieved the conditions needed to attract massive investment in productive facilities—including external currency convertibility, price stability, and political stability—and they are providing effective tax incentives designed to accelerate investment and growth. We cannot, therefore, afford to stand by and do nothing, or put off affirmative action to a later day. We need to increase our investment in machinery and equipment now—delay can only place greater strains on

From a statement of Honorable Douglas Dillon, Secretary of the Treasury, to the United States Senate Finance Committee on the Revenue Act of 1962.

our international payments position and put off the achievement of the rate of growth we must achieve if we are to meet our domestic and international commitments and provide jobs for our ever-increasing labor force.

Machinery and equipment expenditures—the type of business capital expenditure which is basic to the creation of new products and which also makes the most direct contribution to cost-cutting, productivity, and efficiency—constitute a smaller percentage of the gross national project in the United States than in any major industrial nation of the world. In recent years we have devoted less than 6 per cent of our GNP (less than 5 per cent in 1961) to this type of vital capital outlay, only half the proportion devoted to this purpose by West Germany, only three-fourths that of the United Kingdom, and about 60 per cent as much as the combined average of the European members of the OECD. Perhaps even more significant is the fact that in the United States this percentage has recently been declining steadily, whereas it has been increasing in these other nations.

Recent studies indicate a close correlation between the ratio of investment in productive equipment to GNP and the rate of economic growth. In view of the relatively small proportion of GNP that has been allocated to investment in machinery and equipment in the United States, it is not surprising to find that the average annual rate of growth (in constant prices) experienced in the United States in the decade of the fifties was only 3 per cent, compared with more than 7 per cent for West Germany, and with a range of 4 to 6 per cent for most other industrial countries of Western Europe. In order to minimize unemployment, to satisfy the desire of our people for rising standards of living, to meet our defense and other domestic and international obligations, and to demonstrate the vitality of our free economy, we must achieve a higher rate of growth. This we cannot do unless we achieve a more satisfactory rate of capital formation.

We cannot hope to achieve the increased rate of capital formation necessary to more rapid economic growth and full employment unless we bring our tax treatment of capital investment into line with the standards which our European competitors have used so successfully over the past decade. To attain this result the administration is pursuing a two-pronged course in the area of depreciation. One step involves administrative action to modernize depreciation guidelines in keeping with the statutory provision of a "reasonable allowance" for depreciation, including obsolescence. In addition to more realistic recognition of obsolescence and technological trends, the Treasury aims to achieve a simpler, more flexible system of depreciation.

The revised depreciation guidelines, to be announced in late spring of this year, will constitute the first really major change in the administration of depreciation since the early 1930's. The establishment of a modern depreciation system which takes account of the current faster tempo of obsolescence will help to stimulate investment in this country. But, I must emphasize, the shortening of depreciable lives to a fully realistic basis will not bring American industry abreast of its foreign competitors. For all the other major industrialized nations of the free world provide for either the use of unrealistically short lives for depreciation purposes, a practice which distorts income and cost statements, or for special initial allowances or investment allowances which supplement regular depreciation charges, or for a combination of two or more of these incentives.

The percentage of the cost of an asset that may be deducted in the first year ranges from 20 per cent in West Germany to 43.4 per cent in Japan compared with as low as 10.5 per cent in the United States. For the first five years of the life of the asset, the relevant proportion falls within the range of 62 to 70 per cent for West Germany, Japan, and the United Kingdom, between 70 and 80 per cent for Canada and France, and 85 to as much as 100 per cent for Belgium, Italy, the Netherlands, and Sweden. In sharp contrast, the applicable percentage in the United States is 42.7 under the present average Bulletin "F" life and 51.1 per cent for the most commonly used fifteen-year life.

Even a drastic downward revision of depreciable lives beyond anything that can be justified by realistic asset lives would still not bring capital allowances in the United States to a level comparable with that permitted by our foreign competitors. Should our overall administrative revision of depreciation bring about reductions in guideline lives as large as those which were found appropriate for the textile industry, not more than a quarter of the current gap between depreciation practices here and abroad will be closed. Administrative modernization of depreciation simply cannot do the job. The reason is simple. Realistic depreciation cannot be expected to produce depreciation chargeoffs equal to the special incentive provisions in general use abroad. Nor can it provide the additional incentive which the experience of other industrialized countries has demonstrated is needed to broaden and deepen the flow of investment into new, more efficient equipment. The combination of both the forthcoming modernization of depreciation guidelines and a special incentive such as the investment credit contained in the bill before you is required if U.S. business firms are to be placed on substantially equal footing with their foreign competitors in this respect. It is essential to our competitive position in markets, both here, at home, and abroad, that American industry be put on the same basis as foreign industry. Unless this is done, increased imports and decreased exports will unnecessarily add to the burden of our balance-of-payment deficit.

The investment credit will stimulate investment in a number of ways. Because it reduces the net cost of acquiring depreciable assets it increases the rate of profitability. Thus, for example, a ten-year asset that is expected to yield a rate of return after taxes of 5 per cent under straight line or 5.6 per cent under double-declining balance depreciation will, with an 8 per cent investment credit, yield a return of 7.9 per cent per year. This represents an increase in profitability of more than 40 per cent (for a 7 per cent credit the 7.9 and 40 per cent become 7.6 and 35 per cent). An increase of this magnitude will provide a major stimulus to business firms to replace older, less efficient machinery and equipment and, in the process, incorporate the most recent technological developments into productive facilities.

Investment decisions are influenced as well by the availability of funds. Since the credit will increase the flow of cash available for investment, it will stimulate investment through this effect as well as through its effect on profitability. The increased cash flow will be particularly important for new and smaller firms, which do not have ready access to the capital markets and whose growth is often restrained by a lack of capital funds.

Still another way in which the credit may be expected to stimulate investment is through a reduction in the payoff period for investment in a particular asset, which is one measure of the risk associated with any investment. This reduction in risk, coupled with the higher rate of profitability and increased cash flow, will shift the margin at which positive decisions to investment are made and will help to restore to past levels the proportion of our annual output that is devoted, through investment in machinery and equipment, to building the strength, vitality, and competitive force of the American economy.

Another interesting comparison may be made, one that should intrigue those who favor a low-interest rate as a primary investment stimulus. An 8 per cent investment credit reduces the gross financing costs of a ten-year asset as much as would a reduction of the interest rate from 5 to 3⅓ per cent, for a fifteen-year asset from 5 to 3⅔ per cent. But the credit does not entail the balance of payments and other difficulties that would accompany a concerted effort to bring long-term interest rates down by such a large extent.

Some critics of the investment credit have suggested that we should approach the problem of increasing investment through tax changes by giving first priority to measures designed to add to consumer demand. An increase in consumer demand will, of course, induce additional investment, but this is not the only way in which the level of investment may be raised and it would be wrong to place our entire reliance on this approach. This is because investment induced by consumer demand suggests primarily expansion using existing kinds of equipment and techniques, rather than more efficient and larger quantities of capital per worker and, therefore, greater productivity. We cannot be content merely with the level of capital formation that will result from response to increased consumer demand. We must have both more capital equipment per unit of output and increased demand for that output. Thus a higher rate of growth requires a more rapid accumulation of productive facilities than would be forthcoming if investment were induced solely by an increase in final demand. The American economy now is much in need of modernization of its capital equipment which, in the technological environment of the 1960's, requires an increase in the ratio of capital to output. One of the important means of achieving a higher rate of economic growth lies precisely in increasing this ratio, and a direct approach to investment incentives is needed to accomplish this. We must increase the overall attractiveness of investment at any given volume of consumer demand in order that our productivity and growth may be maximized.

With this objective in mind, the credit should be viewed primarily as a means of encouraging the modernization of industrial mining, agricultural, and other equipment, increasing the productivity of the American economy by adding to the quantity and quality of capital available per worker, and increasing the relative attractiveness of investment at home compared with investment abroad.

Those who are properly concerned about the existing gap between current and full employment output urge that this gap should be filled by expansion of consumer demand. But the increase in overall demand required to bring the economy closer to full employment need not consist solely of an increase in consumer demand. Increased investment adds equally to aggregate demand, and in the transition to full employment the rising aggregate demand due to increased investment will, by transmitting itself through the economy, add substantially to consumer demand.

Moreover, in this transition period the total increase in demand—generated by increased investment but including additional outlays on consumer goods and services—will far exceed any overall increase in capacity. Thus the credit will contribute significantly to our objective of achieving a higher level of employment. It should be clearly noted that the increased productive capacity resulting from a more rapid rate of capital formation will also in the long run make possible for higher levels of consumption.

Another objection to the investment credit stems from concern about our ability to maintain full utilization of the increased productive capacity after it has been acquired. I believe that this concern reflects a viewpoint that is far too pessimistic. The underlying forces of expansion in our economy are strong and will be strengthened further by the enactment of the investment credit. The substantial anticipated increase in the labor force in the years ahead provides a challenge and an opportunity, if the necessary tools of production are forthcoming, for a more rapid rate of economic growth than we have experienced in recent history. I am confident that this administration will take such steps as are needed to maintain the required level of total demand. The economic effects of the investment credit will make its task easier. It is in the context of this approach to public policy that the merits of the investment credit must be appraised.

Another criticism which was heard frequently last year was based on a misunderstanding. This was the thought that the credit is a temporary remedy for recession or that it would be somehow offset by more restrictive administration of depreciation. The arguments I have made for the credit clearly reveal that such legislation must be a permanent part of our tax code if we are to meet foreign competition, and our administrative action in the textile field is a harbinger of what is being prepared for other fields—more liberal rather than more restrictive administrative action.

Finally there has been the criticism that holds that the credit is a form of subsidy which other incentive measures are not and that it will not be sufficiently effective as a means of increasing investment. Those who hold this view, including the National Association of Manufacturers, usually favor the acceleration of depreciation beyond what is justified on the basis of realistic accounting. Careful study and consideration of a wide variety of alternatives to the investment credit show, however, that all of these alternatives, without exception, share the same characteristic of giving the investor in equipment a monetary reward beyond what he would receive on the basis of realistic accounting. The element of subsidy or incentive is equally present in all of them. We have chosen the credit primarily because it increases the profitability of investment far more per dollar of revenue cost than any of the other alternatives. For example, the first 5 years' revenue cost of a 20 per cent initial allowance would exceed that of an 8 per cent investment credit by about $1 billion, but the allowance would increase the profitability of investment in a ten-year asset by less than 10 per cent, compared with more than 40 per cent for the investment credit. Even a 40 per cent initial allowance, the cost of which over the next five years would be more than twice as great as the cost of the credit, would have an appreciably smaller effect on profitability for assets with expected useful lives of up to twenty years.

Similar conclusions emerge from our analysis of such incentives as triple-declining balance depreciation and across-the-board percentage increases in depreciation allowances. In addition all of these alternatives which go beyond realistic depreciation suffer from a number of important disadvantages which are not associated with the investment credit. Unrealistically high depreciation charges tend to distort income accounting and produce higher costs for tax and, in the case of a great number of firms, book purposes. Such higher costs may frequently be reflected in higher prices. Since they also cost the government more and provide a lesser stimulus to investment, it seems clear that the investment credit is the best way in which to supply the additional incentive that is so badly needed.

DOMESTIC ECONOMIC POLICIES FOR THE MID-1960's

The Council of Economic Advisers

By 1963 the Administration had decided that investment stimulus could not move the economy to full employment and proposed a general personal and corporate income tax reduction. In the 1963 Annual Report, the Council of Economic Advisers examines how the tax cut will stimulate private spending, the relation between public and private deficits and surpluses, the role of automatic stabilizers, and the past history of using tax reductions to stimulate demand.

TAX REVISION: IMPACT ON OUTPUT AND EMPLOYMENT

Tax reduction will directly increase the disposable income and purchasing power of consumers and business, strengthen incentives and expectations, and raise the net returns on new capital investment. This will lead to initial increases in private consumption and investment expenditures. These increases in spending will set off a cumulative expansion, generating further increases in consumption and investment spending and a general rise in production, income and employment.

Initial Effects: Consumption

Effects on disposable income

The proposed reduction in personal income tax rates will directly add to the disposable income of households. In addition, the reduction in corporate tax rates will increase the after tax profits of corporations as a result of which corporations may be expected to increase their dividend payments. The initial effect on the disposable income of households

From the *Economic Report of the President together with the Annual Report of the Council of Economic Advisers,* January 1963.

resulting from the entire program of tax reductions should be approximately $9 billion, at current levels of income.

Consumer response to increase in disposable income

The ratio of total consumption expenditures to total personal disposable income has in each recent calendar year fallen within the range of 92 to 94 per cent. Although there are lags and irregularities from quarter to quarter or even year to year, the change in personal consumption expenditures has in the past, after a few quarters, averaged roughly 93 per cent of any change in personal disposable income. On this basis, the initial addition to consumer expenditures associated with tax reductions would be on the order of $8 billion, although all would not be spent at once.

Additions to after-tax incomes resulting from tax reduction are likely to be spent in the same way as other additions to income. The largest part of the proposed tax reduction will be reflected in reduced withholding of taxes from wages and salaries, and therefore in larger wage and salary checks; thus, it will be indistinguishable from additional income arising from wage or salary increases, greater employment, or longer hours of work. Similarly, part of the reduced corporate taxes will be passed along to stockholders in increased dividend checks. Stockholders will not be able to identify the source of their additional dividends. Tax reduction dollars carry no identifying label, and there is no reason to expect recipients to treat them differently from other dollars. Recent experience with tax reduction demonstrates clearly that additions to disposable income from this source are spent as completely as any other additions.

It is sometimes suggested that tax reductions which add only a few dollars to the weekly pay check of the typical worker would do little good even if the money was spent, since the amounts involved would not be large enough to permit major expenditures—sway on washing machines or automobiles. Instead, the money would be "frittered away" on minor expenditures and would do little good for the economy. But all purchases lead to production which generates income and provides employment. Therefore, the purpose of tax reduction is achieved when the proceeds are spent on any kind of goods or services.

Actually, of course, tax reduction which expands take-home pay even by a relatively small amount each week or month may induce recipients to purchase durable goods or houses of higher quality, since the increased income would permit them to handle larger monthly installment payments. It may even induce a rearrangement of expenditure patterns and thus bring about purchases of durable goods that would not otherwise be made.

Initial Effects: Investment

Investment is a more volatile element than consumption in national expenditure. The timing and magnitude of its response to tax changes is less predictable. But a cut in tax rates on business income will stimulate spending on new plants and new machinery in two ways. First, it will strengthen investment incentives by increasing the after-tax profits that businessmen can expect to earn on new productive facilities. Second, it will add to the supply of internal funds, a large part of which is normally reinvested in the business (though part of this effect may initially be offset by the proposed acceleration of corporate tax payments).

Since the largest part of business investment is made by corporations, the proposed cuts in the corporate income tax are especially significant. But investments of unincorporated businesses will also be encouraged by cuts in personal income tax rates, especially in the upper brackets.

Two important reforms affecting the taxation of business income designed to stimulate investment in plant and equipment were put into effect during 1962: the new depreciation guidelines and the investment tax credit.

Evidence to date clearly indicates that these measures are already stimulating some capital spending that would not otherwise have taken place. The impact of the 1962 actions and the 1963 proposals to reduce taxes on business will, of course, differ from company to company and industry to industry, depending in part on the adequacy of their internal funds and their levels of capacity utilization. Though the speed of response may vary, industry after industry will begin to feel pressure on its capital facilities and funds as markets for its products are expanded by the 1963 tax program.

Furthermore, there are many individual companies for which the supply of internal funds is a constraint on investment, and many others that do not have excess capacity. Moreover, it is estimated that some 70 per cent of the investment in plant and equipment is for modernization and replacement rather than expansion, that is, it is designed to produce new or better products, or to reduce production costs rather than primarily to expand productive capacity. For this large segment of capital spending, the stronger inducement to invest provided by the business tax changes already adopted and those now proposed will translate much more readily into actual purchases of plant and equipment.

As production expands and existing capacity is more fully utilized, the depreciation guidelines and the investment tax credit and the new business tax reductions will provide an even stronger stimulus to investment.

Cumulative Expansion: The Consumption Multiplier

Tax reduction will start a process of cumulative expansion throughout the economy. If the economy is already undergoing slow expansion, this cumulative process will be superimposed upon it. The initial increases in spending will stimulate production and employment, generating additional incomes. The details and timing of this process will vary from industry to industry. The first impact may be to draw down inventories rather than to expand production. But as inventories are depleted, retailers will quickly expand orders. As manufacturers' sales rise in response and their own inventories of finished goods decline, they will activate idle production lines, hire additional workers, place orders for materials and components. Thus the expansion will spread to other industries, leading to further expansion of production, employment, and orders.

Expanded sales mean increased profits. Increased employment means greater wage and salary income. Each additional dollar's worth of gross production necessarily generates a dollar of additional gross income.

But expansion does not proceed without limit. A considerable fraction of the value of gross production is shared with governments or becomes part of corporate retained earnings and does not become part of consumers' after-tax income. Some of the increase goes to pay additional excise and other indirect business taxes. Typically, when GNP is rising toward potential, corporate profits increase by about one-fourth of the rise in GNP. But a substantial part of this increase in profits is absorbed by federal and state corporate income taxes, and another part is ordinarily retained by the corporations. Only the remainder is passed on to the households in dividend payments. Part of the additional wage and salary incomes associated with added production is absorbed by higher social security contributions. At the same time, increased employment means a drop in payments of unemployment insurance benefits.

When all of these "leakages" are taken into account, a little less than two-thirds of an additional dollar of GNP finds its way into the before-tax incomes of consumers in the form of wages, dividends, and other incomes. Part is absorbed by personal taxes, federal, state, and local. The increase in personal disposable income is 50 to 55 per cent. Of this amount a small fraction—about 7 per cent—is set aside in personal saving, and the remainder—about 93 per cent—is spent on consumption, as indicated earlier. Thus, out of each additional dollar of GNP, initially generated by the tax cut, roughly half ends up as added consumption expenditure. But the process does not stop here.

The additional expenditure on consumption that is brought about by the rise in GNP generates, in its turn, further production, which generates additional incomes and consumption, and so on, in a continuous sequence of expansion which economists call the "multiplier process." The "multiplier" applicable to the initial increase in spending resulting from tax reduction, with account taken of the various leakages discussed above, works out to roughly two. Lags in the process of expansion will spread this increase in GNP over time, but studies of the relationships between changes in disposable income, consumption, and production of consumer goods suggest that at least half of the total stimulus of an initial increase in disposable income is realized within six months of that increase.

Cumulative Expansion: The Investment Response

Tax reduction will also have important cumulative indirect effects on investment in inventories and in fixed productive facilities. These effects are much more difficult to predict than the induced effects on consumption.

Inventory investment

The stocks of goods that businessmen wish to hold depend upon current and expected rates of sales and production and the volume of new and unfilled orders, as well as on price expectations and other factors. An expansion of aggregate demand can be expected to raise business inventory targets. Production for inventory will generate further increases in demand and income over and above the multiplier effects discussed above, and will in turn induce further increases in consumption spending.

Inventory investment is volatile, and induced inventory accumulation can add significantly to the expansionary effects of tax reduction within a few months. At the same time, it should be recognized that inventory investment is exceedingly difficult to forecast. As the increase in production and sales tapers off, stocks and the rate of inventory investment will be correspondingly adjusted.

Business investment in plant and equipment

A tax reduction large enough to move the economy toward full employment will also stimulate business investment in plant and equipment. General economic expansion will reinforce the initial stimulus to investment of cuts in business taxes. In the first place, narrowing the gap between actual and potential output—now estimated at $30 to $40 billion—will increase the utilization of existing plant and equipment. As excess capacity declines, more and more businesses will feel increasing pressure to expand capacity. At the same time, increases in the volume of sales and in productivity will raise corporate profits—in absolute terms, relative to GNP, and as a rate of return on investment. Internal funds available for investment will rise, while at the same time higher rates of return on existing capital will cause businessmen to raise their estimates of returns on new investment. When investment incentives are strengthened by rising demand, internal funds are more consistently translated into increased investment than when markets are slack.

Residential construction

The demand for housing depends on growth in the number of families, on the existing stock of houses, and on the cost and availability of mortgage credit. But housing demand also responds, to some extent, to changes in disposable income. Thus, tax reduction will have some direct effect on residential construction. And as production, employment, and income generally expand, the demand for new homes can be expected to increase further. This increase will, in turn, reinforce the other expansionary effects of tax reduction.

State and Local Government Expenditures

State and local government units have found it difficult to finance the needed expansion of their activities. Given the present importance of income and sales taxes in state and local tax systems, government revenues at the state and local level expand automatically as GNP rises. The additional state-local revenues generated by economic expansion will assist these governments to meet their pressing needs. Moreover, since federal tax liabilities are deductible under many state income tax laws, reduction in federal tax rates will automatically generate some further addition to state-local tax revenues. Finally, a reduction in federal taxes will enlarge the tax base available to state and local government units and may make it easier for them to raise rates or impose new taxes.

Undoubtedly, some of the added state-local tax revenues will be used either to retire existing debt or to reduce current borrowing rather than to increase expenditures. Whether the net result will be expansionary will depend upon whether the proportion of additional tax revenues spent on goods and services by state and local government units is such as to strengthen the aggregate impact of federal tax reduction on income and employment, the federal tax program will ease, to some extent, the problems of these units in obtaining revenues needed to finance urgent public activities, such as education, transportation facilities, and urban development.

Summary of Effects on GNP

Tax reductions for consumers will have initial direct effect on the demand for goods and services, consumers raise their spending level to reflect their higher after-tax incomes. Corporate tax reductions and the lower tax rates applicable to the highest personal income brackets will stimulate investment directly, through raising the rate of return on new investments and providing additional funds for their financing. Some of the tax reforms will also have a directly stimulating effect on productive investment.

These direct or initial effects on spending would occur even if total output, employment, and incomes remained unchanged. But the increased spending cannot fail to increase total output, employment, and incomes. And as activity responds to the initially increased level of spending, cumulative impacts begin to develop in which the several elements interact to carry the expansion far beyond its initial point.

The higher incomes which consumers receive from the added production of both consumer and capital goods will lead to a further step-up in the rate of spending, creating further increases in incomes and spending. The same expansion process raises rates of capacity utilization, thereby interacting with the initial impact of tax reduction on business incomes to make investment both for modernization and expansion more profitable. This in turn generates higher consumer incomes and more spending, helping to provide the added demand which justifies the higher investment.

If there were no investment stimulus—either initially, or as a result of the cumulative process of expansion—we could expect that GNP would ultimately expand by about $16 billion. If the result were no more than this, the tax reduction would still be abundantly rewarding in terms of greater production, employment, purchasing power, and profits. What will really be given up to produce added output will be only unwanted idleness of workers (whose families have reduced neither their needs nor aspirations) and incomplete utilization of plant and machinery (which have continued to depreciate).

But the pay-off is much more than this purely consumption impact. There is also an investment impact, and each extra dollar of investment that is stimulated should bring roughly another dollar of added consumption and encourage still further investment.

A strong expansion can alter profoundly the whole climate within which investment decisions are made. If not at once, then somewhat later, subtle but significant changes in business attitudes occur in response to the trend in the economic outcome. We have referred earlier to the cautious investment attitudes that more than five years of slack markets generated. This caution did not arise at once in mid-1957, when output first began to fall away from the track of potential expansion. It developed gradually, fed on itself, and in part helped to justify itself. The reverse can and will happen.

DEFICITS AND SURPLUSES—PRIVATE AND PUBLIC

For the economy as a whole, expenditures on final output in any past period must necessarily add up to the value of total gross product or income. Therefore, if any one sector in the economy has incurred a deficit by spending more than it has received in income, some other sector must have incurred a surplus by spending less than it has received. Putting it differently, the sum of all sectoral deficits must be identical with the sum of all surpluses. The problem is to maintain a relationship between the deficits and surpluses of the various sectors that will permit this balance to be reached at a satisfactory level of economic activity— and without a prolonged succession of government deficits. The inter-relationship between the levels of surplus and deficit of various sectors in the economy has been tabulated in the President's Economic Report each year since 1947. It gives an interesting insight into the cyclical behavior of the economy and places fluctuations in the federal deficit or surplus in better perspective.

A federal deficit on national income account means that the government's injections into the stream of income and expenditures through purchases of goods and services and transfer payments exceed its withdrawals through taxes and social insurance contributions. Conversely, a surplus means that its withdrawals exceed its injections. (The way in which the government uses its surplus or finances its deficit may have an important bearing on the level of business or even consumer expenditure.)

For consumers, receipts of disposable income are withdrawals, and outlays for consumption represent injections. Expenditures on residential construction, though usually treated in the national income accounts as business investment, are here assigned to the consumer sector, and depreciation charges on residential property are treated accordingly as gross consumer saving.

State and local governments, as the federal government, withdraw purchasing power from the income stream through taxes, and inject it by purchases of goods and services and by transfer payments. The concept of surplus and deficit is the same as for the federal government. In the case of the foreign sector, imports of goods and services drain purchasing power away to other countries, while exports of goods and services for which payments must be made to the United States constitute injections.

For business firms, retained earnings and depreciation allowances (gross saving) are withdrawals from the gross income stream, while expenditures for fixed and inventory investment are injections. A "deficit," in these terms, exists if investment exceeds gross saving. Thus defined, a "deficit" on capital account does not mean that business is unprofitable —quite the contrary. Borrowing to finance investment in productive plant and equipment that yields a return over time lies at the heart of the growth process of the economy. In years of prosperity, when unemployment is low and capacity is fully utilized, business profits are high and the saving from retained earnings and depreciation allowances is relatively large. But in these years, the inducement to invest in new productive facilities is so strong that it substantially outruns even the large supply of internal saving.

The "budget" of the consumer sector characteristically shows a surplus —an excess of disposable income plus depreciation of houses, over the combined total of personal consumption expenditures and residential construction. Indeed, during the period 1947-62, the consumer sector was in surplus in every year except 1947. The average surplus in that period was about $6.5 billion.

State and local governments have had deficits in eleven of the entire sixteen years under review. Their deficits have been relatively small, averaging a little less than a billion dollars in the last few years. The foreign sector has had an excess of current purchases from the United

States over sales to the United States in nine of the sixteen years, and for the whole period the excess of purchases averaged a little less than a billion dollars a year. This excess of purchases is a deficit for purposes of the U.S. national income accounts.

Characteristically, the business and federal government sectors combined show a deficit, which offsets a consolidated surplus in the remaining sectors. However, the only two sectors whose deficits and surpluses exhibit fluctuations clearly related to changes in the general level of business activity are the business sector and the federal government.

The budget of the business sector exhibits surpluses or small deficits in years of recession and slack, moves toward deficit as the economy expands, and commonly achieves a substantial deficit in years of prosperity and low unemployment. Consequently, it is in prosperous years, such as 1947, 1948, 1950, 1951, 1952, 1955, 1956, and 1957, that the business sector has had large deficits on capital account. It is in those years that business raises large amounts of funds on the capital market and uses the surpluses of other sectors. On the other hand, when there is substantial unemployment and unutilized capacity, as in the recession years 1949 and 1954 and the years 1958-62, the inducement to invest tends to be so weak that investment spending falls, even relative to the reduced levels of gross retained earnings, and the business sector budget shows only a small deficit or even a surplus.

The federal budget shows a reverse pattern. It consistently moves toward a surplus as the economy expands and toward a deficit as it contracts. These movements are mainly a passive result of the operation of the automatic fiscal stabilizers, though they reflect also active measures of fiscal policy aimed at minimizing economic fluctuations. As a general rule, the federal government has had budget surpluses in years when the unemployment rate has averaged less than 5½ per cent of the labor force and budget deficits in years when the rate has exceeded that figure. The only exceptions to this rule between 1947 and 1962 were the years in 1952 and 1953 when the requirements of the Korean war forced very high military expenditures in a time of prosperity and low unemployment, and the year 1960 when a deliberate contraction of federal expenditures cut short recovery from the 1957-58 recession while unemployment was still high. On the other hand, in years when unemployment has exceeded 5½ per cent, the business sector has had an average deficit of less than $2 billion, whereas in years in which unemployment has been less than 5½ per cent the business sector deficit has averaged $9 billion.

It is evident that the deficit or surplus in the business sector is related to the surplus or deficit in the federal government sector. More important, it is a major determinant of the total level of expenditures and hence of economic activity. When capital spending is sluggish, the over-all level of expenditure, and hence income, is likely to be unsatisfactory. A passive deficit in the federal sector will occur. But this, in itself, cannot provide the new inducement to investment that will restore full employment and in the process permit the federal government a surplus in its own accounts.

The business sector cannot, of course, be expected to run large deficits merely in order to maintain high levels of economic activity. General economic stabilization is a responsibility of the federal government, not of private business organizations. Unavoidable fluctuations in private demand make it almost certain that the federal budget will show deficits in some years. But the way to avoid chronic federal deficits and achieve surpluses with reasonable frequency is to pursue active federal policies —including budget and tax policies—designed to keep the economy operating continuously at high levels of employment and capacity utilization.

Prospects for the Future

There are many reasons for confidence that, once full employment is restored by fiscal action, the private sectors will once again find it to their advantage to increase investment and incur deficits sufficient to generate a balance in the federal account—that the private economy will find new buoyancy which will make surpluses possible and appropriate.

The weakness of fixed business investment in recent years has reflected—and in turn reinforced—the slow and uncertain growth of aggregate demand. Greater utilization of existing capacity may not immediately yield a burst of investment activity. Business which expanded capacity in 1955-57 in the expectation of expanding markets and reaped only a harvest of higher overhead costs may be hesitant to bet again on sustained prosperity. But as strong markets are restored and maintained, business confidence can and will revive. Private investment will then be once again the primary force for economic growth. Structural factors will favor this development. For example, beginning in the second half of the 1960's demographic conditions were ripe for one of the strongest and most prolonged booms in residential construction this country has ever known. The vast research and development effort of

American industry will yield new techniques and new products which will be profitable to install in steadily expanding markets.

The historical record of the American economy—like that of every industrialized country—exhibits an irregular sequence of periods of strong and buoyant demand, alternating with intervals of weakness and slack. The reasons for this irregularity are many: massive innovations like the automobile or electrification, the opening or closing of new territories, bursts of population growth, the temporary drying-up of profitable investment opportunities. History teaches that all such periods end. The natural tendency to extrapolate the recent past ought not to blind us to the likelihood that the weakness of the past few years will sooner or later be transformed into strength. But if we fail to do what is needed now, the transformation may be longed delayed.

PASSIVE FISCAL POLICY AND AUTOMATIC STABILIZATION

Any weakening in private spending will reduce incomes, causing tax revenues to fall and transfer payments to rise. Thus disposable incomes will decline less than pre-tax incomes and will be partly cushioned against the decline in private demand. In effect, the impact of the decline in private income is shared with the federal government which does not shrink its purchases when its income falls. The greater the extent to which a fall in government revenues cushions the decline in private incomes, the less the flow of spending for output will be curtailed.

Automatic stabilization operates in reverse when private demand increases. Additional income is generated, but part of it is siphoned out of the spending stream in higher tax payments and lower transfers. Disposable incomes therefore rise less than incomes before taxes, and the spending and re-spending is limited and damped.

Thus the tax-and-transfer response narrows fluctuations in income caused by irregulartiies in the strength of demand. The sharper the response of tax collections to changes in GNP, the stronger the stabilization effect. Although the tax-and-transfer response cannot prevent or reverse a movement in GNP, it can and does limit the extent of cumulative expansions and contractions. At least with respect to contractions, this is clearly an important service to the economy.

Automatic fiscal stabilizers have made a major contribution in limiting the length and severity of postwar recessions. Each of the four postwar recessions—1948-49, 1953-54, 1957-58, and 1960-61—has been both short and mild. The decline in real GNP from its peak to its trough has ranged from a high of 4.4 per cent in 1957-58 to a low of 2.1 per cent in 1960-61, and the duration of the recessions has varied from nine to thirteen months. Changes in disposable personal income from quarter to quarter have been much smaller than changes in GNP. Although GNP changes were frequently negative (in each of the postwar recessions), disposable income fell in only one quarter in the entire postwar period. This relative stability of personal disposable income has been mainly due to the automatic fiscal stabilizers, together with the tendency of corporations to maintain their dividends at the expense of retained earnings during recessions. The maintenance of disposable incomes has prevented sharp declines in consumer expenditures. The resulting stability in markets for consumer goods, which constitute by far the largest component of final demand, has prevented any drastic collapse in business investment in fixed capital.

Automatic fiscal stabilizers increase the stability of the economy. Stability is a desirable thing for an economy that is balanced where it wants to be. Thus, an economy operating, on the average, at high levels of output and employment benefits from a tax-and-transfer system highly responsive to changes in output and income, as a cushion against sharp movements of aggregate demand either toward inflation or toward recession.

However, in 1963—with the American economy laboring well below its potential rate of output—automatic stabilization becomes an ambiguous blessing. The protection it gives against cumulative downward movements of output and employment is all the more welcome. But its symmetrical "protection" against upward movements becomes an obstacle on the path to full employment, throttling expansion well before full employment is reached.

Under such conditions, high employment can be restored—as is being proposed under the 1963 tax program—by a reduction in taxes. When this is done the need is not primarily to lessen the responsiveness of tax receipts to changes in GNP. Rather the whole schedule of taxes should be lowered—so that, at any given GNP, taxes siphon off less private purchasing power—while leaving the response of tax receipts to changes in GNP about as great as before. To be sure, it is almost impossible to lower taxes without lessening to some degree their sensitivity to changes in GNP. But the purpose of such a change should be to lower the level of taxes—and hence their persistent drag on purchasing power—rather than to reduce their automatic countercyclical response.

Tax Cuts to Aid Recovery

Just as we have had postwar experience with automatic stabilization, we have had experience with active tax cuts which served positively to increase demand. These experiences are of interest in the present context.

In two of the postwar recessions—1948-49 and 1953-54—tax cuts helped to check the decline and to spur the ensuing recovery. Neither of the tax cuts is an example of deliberate countercyclical fiscal action, but both had important expansionary effects which came when they were needed.

Under the Revenue Act of 1948, which was passed by the Congress in April, taxes were reduced by $4.7 billion. While at the time, the tax cut appeared inappropriately timed—few observers were predicting recession—when the recession of 1949 in fact occurred, it turned out to be fortunate that the tax cut had been legislated. The cut was retroactive to January 1, 1948, and as a result refunds were exceptionally large in mid-1949. The upturn began in October 1949. In addition to the tax cut, there was a significant increase in federal expenditures in late 1948 associated with the introduction of the Marshall Plan. This also helped to mitigate the recession. The economy was further stimulated in the expansion phase by the heavy increases in placement of military orders associated with the Korean War, which began in June 1950. As a result of the tax cut and the increased expenditures, together with the effects of the automatic stabilizers, the recession was short and mild, and the ensuing expansion was strong. By the first quarter of 1951, unemployment had been reduced to 3.5 per cent of the labor force.

As a result of the rapid expansion, by the second quarter of 1950, federal tax liabilities as shown in the national income accounts had risen substantially above the levels that prevailed at the time taxes were cut in the second quarter of 1948.

Taxes also were cut during the recession of 1953-54. Effective January 1, 1954, the excess profits tax was repealed, and personal income tax rates were reduced. Excise taxes were reduced on April 1, and further tax reductions for both individuals and corporations were embodied in the Internal Revenue Code of 1954. These measures are estimated to have reduced federal revenues by about $6.1 billion (seasonally adjusted annual rate) in the first half of 1954. Further cuts which went into effect later brought the revenue loss on a full-year basis to about $7.4 billion. These cuts in personal and corporate income and excise taxes were partially offset, however, by an increase of about $1.4 billion (annual rate) in OASI contributions, which became effective on January 1, 1954. For the most part, the tax reductions in 1954 were part of a program of tax reform and were not viewed primarily as fiscal policy measures aimed at countering the recession. Yet as a result of the tax cuts that became effective at the beginning of 1954, disposable personal income and personal consumption expenditures turned up in the first quarter, while personal income and GNP were still declining. It is generally agreed that the recession ended in August. Tax reduction, together with an easy monetary policy which made a plentiful supply of funds available to finance a strong expansion of housing and automobile demand, helped to shorten the recession and to invigorate the ensuing expansion which brought unemployment down to 4.2 per cent of the labor force by the third quarter of 1955.

As a result of the expansion, by the first quarter of 1955 total federal tax liabilities, as shown in the national income accounts, had risen significantly above the level that prevailed in the fourth quarter of 1953 before the tax cuts were put into effect.

While the tax cuts of 1954 helped considerably in rescuing the economy from the recession, it should be recognized that had they gone into effect earlier, the recession of 1953-54 might have been completely avoided. Government expenditures (principally defense spending) were cut by nearly $11 billion between mid-1953 and mid-1954. The tax cuts took effect six months after expenditures began to fall. As it was, fiscal policy, taken as a whole, was contractionary in this period and was a major cause of the recession. The federal deficit as shown in the national income and product accounts was $7.0 billion (seasonally adjusted annual rate) in the second quarter of 1953 when the recession began. By the fourth quarter the operation of the automatic stabilizers associated with the decline in economic activity had increased the deficit to $11.8 billion despite significant cuts in expenditures. The deficit dropped to $10.6 billion in the first quarter of 1954, and as a result of sharp cuts in expenditures, to $5.4 billion in the second quarter despite the tax reductions that went into effect in the first half of 1954.

Private scholars who have studied the period have estimated that if the economy had continued to operate at the same rate of unemployment that prevailed in the second quarter of 1953, the budget deficit would have dropped from $7.0 billion in that quarter to $3.8 billion in the fourth quarter of 1953 and would have shifted to a surplus of $3.0 billion by the second quarter of 1954. This represents a shift of $10 billion between the peak of the previous recovery and the trough of the recession. It is an approximate measure of the net contractive effect of active fiscal policy during this period.

FISCAL POLICY IN THE 1930's

During the 1930's, America had its longest uninterrupted experience with budget deficits. Their persistence, their relatively large size in comparison with GNP, and their association with an unprecedented unemployment rate (averaging 18.2 per cent from 1930-39) have sometimes been interpreted as demonstrating the futility of expansionary fiscal policy.

The 1930's were a tragic period in the nation's history. The "Great Depression," the causes of which are still not fully diagnosed, produced a tremendous "gap" between actual and potential output—not the 6 per cent average of recent years but about 40 per cent during much of the period. In such an abnormal situation, it is perhaps too much to expect that fiscal policy alone could have fully offset a prolonged failure of the private economy to generate strong expansionary forces.

But in fact, active fiscal policy was not employed vigorously, consistently, or with proper timing. And whatever constructive impact fiscal policy may have had was largely offset by restrictive monetary policies and by institutional failures—failures that could never again occur because of fundamental changes made during and since the 1930's.

Briefly summarized, the facts are these:

(1) Fiscal policy was moderately expansionary for the decade as a whole. Federal expenditures increased substantially, adding to total demand. But most of the effect of this expenditure growth was offset by a series of very heavy tax rate increases, especially in the Revenue Acts of 1932 and 1936. Federal revenues increased by 77 per cent over the decade even with a terribly depressed tax base. If the unemployment rate had stayed at the 1929 level, revenues would have more than doubled. The federal budget changed from a surplus of slightly over $1 billion in 1929 to deficits that would have averaged less than $1 billion over the decade had unemployment been at the same level as in 1929. Of course, because of the collapse of the revenue base, actual deficits were much larger; but these were partly the passive product of depression and partly the reflection of an actively expansionary policy.

(2) At two crucial periods, fiscal policy shifted sharply in a contractionary direction: in 1932-33, and again in 1937-38. In the first period the contractionary policy coincided with and intensified the monetary collapse, and in the second shocked off the 1937 recovery.

(3) State and local government budgets were then much larger than the federal budget, and they were changed in a highly restrictive manner, shifting from a deficit in 1929 to surpluses after 1934.

(4) Unemployment melted away very rapidly when military needs began in 1941 to lead to large budget deficits. Of course, as these expenditures and deficits grew during the war, they not only restored full employment but became a serious inflationary danger. But this wartime overdose of expansionary fiscal medicine should not obscure the fact that more moderate dosages in the early stages quickly solved an unemployment problem which had seemed insoluble for ten years. This was not because the expenditures happened to be military in nature—any expenditures, private or public, on the same scale would have expended demand and put men back to work.

SOME CONCLUSIONS FROM PAST EXPERIENCE

Several conclusions emerge from the preceding review.

The automatic stabilization which our present fiscal system provides is a powerful weapon to damp cyclical movements of output and employment. It is one of the factors that has kept the U.S. economy free from major depressions in the postwar period.

The postwar record shows that deliberate tax cuts can have a counter-cyclical impact, encouraging recovery by stimulating private demand. The experience reviewed above shows how in two cases tax reduction contributed in this manner to recovery from recession. The fact that these tax changes came at times when they helped to check recession and encourage recovery was, however, largely accidental.

The 1948 tax reduction was intended as a permanent one, reflecting the postwar decline of military expenditures. The 1954 tax cuts were also intended as a permanent adjustment to the sharp reductions in government expenditures at the end of the Korean emergency. But a recession will not always coincide with the need for permanent tax reduction. The temporary fluctuations in private demand that are commonly responsible for cyclical movements in business activity thus may call for temporary adjustments in fiscal policy that can be reversed as the need for them recedes.

In 1962 the President proposed two measures for greater fiscal flexibility to meet recessions. These were (a) a proposal that the Congress grant to the President limited authority to initiate temporary reductions in personal income tax rates, subject to congressional approval; and (b) a proposal that the Congress give the President stand-by authority to accelerate and initiate appropriately timed public capital improvements in times of serious unemployment. In his Economic Report the President reaffirmed his support of the principle underlying these two proposals.

A weak private economy can generate very large deficits without receiving a positively stimulating effect from those deficits. The large passive deficits of the 1930's provided examples. More recent examples appear in the experience since 1958. Although the administrative budgets presented for the fiscal years 1958-63 foresaw a surplus in every year, averaging $1.4 billion, the actual outcome has been a deficit in all but one of these years, averaging $5.5 billion. The discrepancy between the Administration's proposed budget and the actual fiscal outcome is, of course, accounted for by two factors: variance between actual and anticipated GNP, and Congressional action modifying both expenditures and taxes. But the major factor explaining these discrepancies was the failure of the economy to attain the GNP that had been anticipated.

Passive deficits are largest when the economy experiences recession. A recession which would reduce the expected GNP gains in fiscal year 1964 by even $15 billion below what they would otherwise be would add almost $5 billion to the deficit.

The experience of the last few years should make it clear that merely to incur deficits is not an appropriate objective of policy. For it is not the deficits as such that provide stimulus. Only reductions in tax rates or increases in expenditures have an actively stimulating role. The passive deficits which are the product of recession or slack, however, have a valuable cushioning function. Nevertheless, it is an appropriate objective of policy to eliminate the deficits that are the product of a recession or a sluggish economy—because of the human and economic waste that is involved in recessions and slack. The proper objectives of policy are full employment and growth, and recessions and slack are the opposites of these.

It is clear that the deficit which a slack economy or recession produces cannot realistically be eliminated by raising tax rates or by reducing government expenditures. Its source is not excessive spending or tax rates that are too low. The attempt to eliminate a deficit by these means would be largely self-defeating. Such a policy would be disastrous for employment, incomes, profits; the deficit would remain; and the role of the dollar as an international currency would be undermined.

Expenditures that are wasteful or represent improper fields for government action (something which only the public, acting through elected representatives, can determine) should surely be eliminated. But unless taxes were simultaneouly reduced by more than expenditures decline, the effect would be contractionary on the economy. The beneficial effect on incentives through lower tax rates might be more than offset by a net loss in demand. A cut in expenditures reduces market demand directly by the full amount of the cut, while an equal reduction in taxes expands market demand by a smaller amount, because a part of the reduction will be added to personal and business saving.

Deficits that result from recession or slack can be eliminated only by restoring and maintaining a vigorous, rapidly growing economy. If the tax system imposes an excessive drag on the economy—through its effects on purchasing power and on incentives—tax rates may be too high relative to expenditures, even though the budget is in deficit. Thus, tax revision, involving both reduction and reform, can not only provide stimulus for growth and prosperity, but can even, as a result, balance the budget or produce surpluses. Recession and slack generate deficits; prosperity and growth balance budgets.

A REPUBLICAN CRITIQUE

Minority Members of the Joint Economic Committee

President Kennedy's tax-cut proposals were delayed for one year in Congress. In the minority report of the Joint Economic Committee the Republican members detail their objections to the President's policies. They do not think that inadequate aggregate demand is a central cause of slow growth or high unemployment and urge a cut in federal expenditures to bring the federal budget into balance. To stimulate growth they wish to concentrate more of the tax reduction in the business sector of the economy. The minority members of the Joint Economic Committee were Senators Jacob Javits, Jack Miller, and Len Jordan, and Representatives Thomas Curtis, Clarence Kilburn, and William Widnall.

The American people have been told by spokesmen for this administration in 1961, when it took over the reins of the federal government, we were in the "valley of recession." The rate of unemployment was 6.7 per cent. We had a "slack" economy, and our annual rate of economic growth was unsatisfactory. Our favorable balance of exports over imports was not what it should be. Farmers were being forced off their farms because they were not receiving "full parity of income." We had a serious balance-of-payments deficit. And our gold supply was rapidly falling to an alarming level.

Now, after two years in office, during which it has had firm control over both Houses of the Congress, by its own definition the administration finds us back in a similar "valley of recession." Our rate of unemployment is 6.1 per cent, notwithstanding the addition of over 186,000 more civilians to the federal payroll and an increase of over 192,000 in the armed services. We are in the grip of "economic lethargy" (as the Chairman of the President's Council of Economic Advisers termed it).

From the *Joint Economic Report on the 1963 Economic Report of the President,* March 1963. U.S. Congress Joint Economic Committee.

Our balance-of-payments deficit was $2.2 billion in 1962 and would have been nearly $700 million larger had it not been for the accelerated repayment of debts owed us by certain foreign governments. Our gold supply has gone down an average of nearly $900 million in each of the last two years to a low as of March 4 of $15.8 billion, and the drain is continuing. With $12 billion of this needed to back up our currency, it is clear that this cannot continue much longer. Potential claims by foreigners against our gold stock amount to over $20 billion. Senator Harry Byrd, Democrat of Virginia, chairman of the Senate Finance Committee, has warned that devaluation of the dollar might be the result. Professor Paul Samuelson, one of the Presidents consultants on economics, recently suggested that the dollar may be *overvalued* and that our policy should be to "alter the parity of the dollar."

The federal debt has increased nearly $14 billion, the consumer price index has increased by over 2 per cent, and general inflation has reduced the purchasing power of our people's money by $14 billion. This record hardly justifies the Presidents assertion that the past two years have brought the greatest record of price stability in the postwar period. At the same time, although there has been some rise in the standard of living, there are millions of less fortunate Americans whose standard of living has not improved or has actually worsened.

Our annual rate of economic growth has been a little over 3 per cent —far short of the administration's goal of 5 per cent.

It is our position that any program of governmental action to improve the economy must be premised on the stable purchasing power of our money if it is to be meaningful. Inflation causes labor to demand increased wages because it cannot make ends meet with the reduced purchasing power of its wages. Escalation clauses in labor-management contracts affecting thousands of workers automatically result in wage increases as the cost of living moves upward. Millions of our senior citizens living on retirement income and savings find that the reduced purchasing power of their money keeps them from an adequate diet and increases the cost of their medical and hospital care.

It is in this setting that we now proceed to evaluate the specific proposals of the administration and to advance our ideas for attaining the meaningful and sustained economic growth which the American people deserve.

A. NATURE OF OUR ECONOMIC PROBLEMS

In our view, the major domestic problem of the present decade is the adjustment required by the increasingly rapid pace of technological change in our society. In his testimony before the House Ways and Means Committee on February 8, 1963, Secretary of Labor W. Willard Wirtz spoke of "a revolution in the replacement of men by machines." This phenomenon is so rapid and profound that a word—automation—has been coined to describe it.

With each passing year, less and less labor is required to produce more of the products of our farms, mines, and factories. As relatively less labor is required to satisfy our basic material needs, more labor—but of a different kind—is called upon to satisfy the preferences that arise out of the desire for a better and fuller life for ourselves and our children.

Rapid technological progress is essential to maintain our economic and military leadership and to provide a higher standard of living for our growing population. But it creates individual hardships and demands difficult and often painful personal and family adjustments.

Automation, for example, creates demands for new and higher skills, but it makes old skills obsolete. In the process, the person with no skill, or with an obsolete skill, or in an area other than where the new jobs are located, becomes increasingly subject to frequent and persistent periods of unemployment.

Rapidly advancing technology also results in new and improved industrial processes and, by creating demands for new products, changes patterns of consumption. Among other results, these developments make obsolete much of our capacity to produce existing products.

Our unemployment problem has been aggravated further by barriers to worker mobility, industrial migration, featherbedding on the part of both management and labor, foreign competition, multiple jobholding by individuals, the movement of workers away from the farm, inadequate attention to the rehabilitation of the physically and mentally handicapped, discrimination based on age, sex, race, and creed, weaknesses in our educational system, particularly in the area of vocational training, and a tax structure which discourages industrial expansion. Compounding the problems caused by the technological revolution and these other factors, we will soon face an explosion in the size of our labor force as the large number of babies born in the 1940's reaches working age.

Clearly the primary challenge of the 1960's is to cease and facilitate the adjustment of our people to these economic forces of change. Technological advances will provide opportunities for a fuller, more satisfying and freer life for all of our people. But it will take imagination and effort to insure that those lacking needed skills or experience, those who are poor in talent and those who suffer discrimination in employment share in the opportunities which these developments will provide. Failure to adjust will bring untold human suffering as well as blunt our efforts to achieve a higher level of sustained economic growth.

We regret that the administration, while proclaiming a New Frontier, has not regarded with sufficient urgency the extent or depth of the adjustments facing us in the decade ahead. Even worse, it has either failed to grasp or has neglected the need to make the nation more fully aware of them.

B. CRITIQUE OF THE ADMINISTRATION'S BASIC ECONOMIC ASSUMPTIONS

The heart of the administration's economic program consists of efforts to increase consumer demand. This would be done by a series of "planned" but "temporary" budget deficits, partly resulting from the proposed tax reduction. Basic to the administration's program is a belief in the efficacy of budget deficits as a remedy for our new economic problems, of which persistent and mounting unemployment and an apparent excess of industrial capacity are but surface symptoms. The administration apparently has abandoned the theory of balancing the budget over the business cycle. It now asserts that we must run deficits in good times and bad until some distant future when federal revenues presumably—or hopefully—will catch up with increasing expenditures.

It is curious that, in spite of the failure of a series of large and steadily increasing budget deficits to stimulate a full recovery from the last cyclical downturn, the administration still retains its faith in the stimulative effect of "temporary" deficits. Interestingly, the current upturn is the only one in the postwar period which has not developed a budget surplus.

The administration claims that deficits are "passive" if caused by a decline in economic activity. Passive deficits, the Council of Economic Advisers has said, do not provide stimulus; only deficits resulting from tax cuts or spending increases stimulate the economy.

If this were the case, the deficits of the past two years of cyclical upturn should have stimulated the economy since they were caused more by rapidly rising federal spending than lagging revenues. Expenditures increased by $13 billion from fiscal 1961 through the estimates for fiscal 1963. At the same time, revenues were increasing by $8 billion. If revenues were lagging, it was only in relation to the sharp increases in federal spending.

We think the administration overemphasizes the importance of fiscal measures to increase consumer demand. More relevant—and less costly in terms of budget impact—are those measures that would sharpen incentives to superior economic performance and thus produce the more vigorous expansion needed to reap the full benefits of the economic revolution now underway.

As for the thesis that the overall magnitude of the federal budget deficit, *per se,* is a measure of governmental stimulus to the economy, it is useful to note an analysis of the relationship between the federal budget (national income accounts basis) and economic activity included in a paper presented to the committee by George Terborgh, research director of the Machinery and Allied Products Institute. Terborgh's analysis shows that there is no general pattern to support the theory that deficits are stimulative and surpluses repressive. In fact, in the postwar period, of fifty-one quarters with a rising gross national product, Terborgh found that twenty-eight were associated with a federal surplus, twenty-three with a deficit. Of thirteen quarters with declining gross national product, twelve were associated with a deficit. The same unstable pattern emerged when the gross national product was compared with the budget position six months earlier.

Neither do the facts bear out the administration's contention that aggregate demand is lagging. From 1947 to 1962 personal consumption expenditures and total government demand for goods and services averaged 84.5 per cent of gross national product. In 1961 the figure was 85.9 per cent and in 1962, 85.7 per cent. During 1961 and 1962 new construction was about 8 per cent of gross national product—or slightly higher than the postwar average. In its 1963 annual report, the Council of Economic Advisers itself acknowledged that the failure of gross national product in 1962 to reach predicted levels was not caused by a shortfall of consumption.

What has fallen behind is the percentage of gross national product accounted for by producers' durable equipment. This averaged 6.1 per cent for the entire postwar period, but stood at 4.9 per cent in 1961 and 5.2 per cent in 1962.

An increase in aggregate demand may be helpful in attacking cyclical unemployment, but this is not the current problem. Our economy has moved in twenty-four months from the low point of the last cyclical downturn—which was relatively minor by postwar standards—and has now reached a new level of gross national product.

Although the nation as a whole is prosperous, too many of our citizens are not sharing in this prosperity. Unemployment from February 1961 through February 1963 declined by only 500,000 (seasonally adjusted). In February, about 4.4 million persons (seasonally adjusted), or 6.1 per cent of the civilian labor force, were still unemployed.

It appears that increases in aggregate demand are having less and less impact in reducing the level of unemployment. We are learning anew that an increase in the demand for commodities does not necessarily translate itself into increased demand for labor, or at least for the labor of the unemployed.

In large part, this reflects structural changes in the economy. The increasing importance of structural unemployment is clearly indicated by the fact that the average duration of unemployment in 1962 (14.7 weeks) was higher, except for one year, than at any time since the end of World War II, including during recession years.

The extent to which obsolete capacity, as opposed to inadequate demand, may have been responsible for the low industrial operating rates of recent years is indicated by the heavy emphasis manufacturers have placed on modernizing their plant and facilities. The fifteenth McGraw-Hill survey of business plans for new plants and equipment showed that since 1958, manufacturing firms have devoted about 70 per cent of their plant and equipment investment to replacement and modernization of obsolete facilities. The need to produce new and improved products more efficiently explains why the steel industry, although operating at an average of 71.8 per cent of capacity from 1957 to 1960, at the same time spent over $5.5 billion on new plant and equipment. The modernization trend in industry is expected to continue at least through 1965. This fact reemphasizes the point made earlier that our major domestic problem is the adjustment of men to new technological conditions.

It is important to remember that excess capacity figures cited to show a lagging economy are averages for all industries. Generally, some industries are operating at or near their preferred rates, while others are operating well below the desired levels. In a dynamic economy both the size and shape of demand are constantly changing. When growth increases demand for products already being produced at capacity levels of existing plant, the mere existence of excess capacity in other industries is irrelevant. Furthermore, it should be clear that increased demand for the products of industries operating at capacity can lead to inflationary pressures even though the overall average indicates the existence of idle capacity.

The administration's general approach to economic issues is based on the assumption that our economy is stagnant, slack, and tired out. It assumes that our economic growth rate has slowed considerably and that there is a growing gap between actual and potential production.

We wish to make clear that the desirability of achieving a higher rate of economic growth is not at issue. A vigorous rate of sustained economic growth facilitates adjustment to the technological revolution. But we submit that the administration has incorrectly diagnosed our problem as one of stagnation. We wish to state briefly, some of the reasons for our disagreement with the administration's basic assumptions.

One trouble with the gap theory is its use of gross national product as the indicator of economic growth. The gross national product is only one measure of economic activity. It does not fully measure true economic growth, by which we mean the attainment of a richer and fuller life for more of our citizens. Gross national product rises rapidly during a war, but no one would call this true economic growth. Indicators of true economic growth, such as increased leisure time, new and improved goods and services on the market, greater longevity, better health, greater opportunities for education and travel, are not reflected, or reflected only incompletely, in the gross national product. By these and other measures, our economy has scored impressive gains in growth in the past decade.

The gross national product analysis is a logical and statistical construct that has no real counterpart in a complex and dynamic economy based on decentralized free choice and initiative. Free enterprise means trial and error, change and adjustment. This is an inevitable aspect of effective economic performance and, in fact, of managerial decisions generally. There is no reason founded on convincing evidence to believe that the complex processes of any economy can work perpetually at an even pace or near some full employment or "potential" trend line.

The fact is that our economy, while beset with problems, is continuing its steady growth. Our diagnosis shows that we are suffering more from growing pains than tired blood.

As we emphasized earlier, this is not to say that we cannot and should not improve our rate of growth. But we cannot encourage faster growth and, at the same time, solve the problems arising from growth by applying a treatment more appropriate to stagnation or cyclical decline.

Our most fundamental criticism of the administration is that its failure to identify the real nature of our economic problems diverts the nation's attention from them and thus delays a genuine solution.

We cannot afford to mark time much longer. Labor's call for a thirty-five-hour week and for industrial sabbaticals, as well as the recent rash of serious labor disputes, make clear that uneasiness about basic changes in the economy are spreading. The administration must lead history, or it will find itself overtaken by it.

C. THE ADMINISTRATION'S TAX PROGRAM

The President has sent to the Congress a program of individual and corporate income tax reduction and reform designed to improve our rate of economic growth and reduce the unemployment rate to 4 per cent (a rate deemed by him to reflect "full employment").

We agree that our federal tax structure discourages, rather than encourages, sound business and business expansion with its attendant employment opportunities. We support reform of our tax structure and rates, but we have several reservations about the administration's program.

1. Inadequacies of Administration Tax Program

We believe that the tax program, even while incurring heavy costs in terms of budget deficits, will fail to remove the tax impediments to growth in sufficient amounts to carry the economy to higher levels of sustained activity. Our reasoning is largely, although not exclusively, based on the three-year stretch-out of the program, on the concentration of the largest and most constructive reductions in the second and third years, and on the excessive emphasis on stimulating consumption at the expense of improvements in our productive plant.

In his testimony before the committee, Dr. Heller conceded that the program would have been somewhat different if the administration lived by economics alone. A number of other witnesses who appeared before the committee expressed doubts about the effectiveness of the program. After two years of recovery, it is altogether possible that counterexpansionary forces might seriously offset any beneficial effects which could flow from the moderate and gradually applied tax reductions.

Whatever one's position on tax reduction, it cannot be justified on the basis of the multiplier theory—as the administration and the majority try to do. The serious problems connected with predicting the multiplier effects of tax cuts were stressed in a statement presented to the committee by the Department of Commerce. As the Department said:

Theoretically the multiplier effects abstract from the numerous other forces which are operating in the economy at any given time. Additional expenditure brought about by a tax cut, for example, must be superimposed upon estimates of the net effect of these forces before a realistic appraisal can be made of the future behavior of the economy subsequent to changes in the tax laws. A tax cut which is too small or which is introduced at a time when the economy is leveling off or even beginning to turn down may not lead automatically to an increase in output. This is the reason why an examination of the past relations involving tax cuts or other multiplier-inducing actions on the subsequent behavior of output is so inconclusive. We find a variety of net effects arising from an expenditure which has multiplier effects; namely, output rising, leveling, and even turning down. To fully appraise such changes in the tax laws or other actions we would have to determine the most likely behavior of the economy in the absence of such changes. This is a difficult task.

There are additional reasons why the administration's program might not do what is expected of it. For example, the effect of tax reduction would be blunted if, contrary to the administration's expectations, consumers saved one or two percentage points more than 7 per cent of total after-tax income. While recent experience indicates that consumers save about this amount of total after-tax income, the savings rate on marginal increases in income is probably greater than 7 per cent. Moreover, the 7 per cent assumption is related to all individuals in the economy. However, many lower income individuals—who bring the average rate down—do not pay taxes. Therefore, the savings rate among those who will obtain the tax reduction undoubtedly is higher than 7 per cent.

The effects of the tax cut also would be largely offset if consumers used a significant part of their tax reduction to pay off existing debt. In addition, a large part of the tax reductions will be offset by the $2 billion increase in the social security payroll tax which has already taken effect this year and by those increases scheduled to take effect in the coming years. Increases in state and local taxes and increases in the consumer price index will further diminish the effect of tax cuts.

We doubt that the administration's fiscal program of moderate and gradually applied tax cuts accompanied by increases in spending will work. The chances of failure are compounded by the administration's almost total neglect of other important actions which are required by the current economic situation. Some of these bear on the question of why there is a drop-off in business investment. Psychological factors, such as business confidence, and economic factors, such as the risk of the rate of return, weigh heavily on investment.

If the administration's program does fail, the nation will be left with a high level of unemployment, a prolonged series of budget deficits, an increase in the economy's inflationary potential, aggravated problems of debt management, and a possible worsening of our balance-of-payments and gold problems.

We believe that our diagnosis of the economy and our recommendations for overcoming the nation's economic problems, both by incentive tax reduction and reform, as well as by other important measures, offer the best choice of policy and should be adopted by the administration.

Our recommendations on the general principles that should govern a tax program for 1963 are as follows:

a. We strongly favor enactment of a permanent reduction in personal and corporate taxes accompanied by expenditure control, noninflationary debt financing, and additional actions to remove impediments to growth. One-half of the annual reduction should take effect in calendar 1963, with the full reduction taking effect in calendar 1964.

b. The precise size of the tax reduction required to substantially reduce impediments to growth without leading to increased inflation is not clear. However, we believe that it must be larger than the $2.7 billion net cut for 1963 proposed by the administration. An annual reduction of from $7 to $8 billion might be about right to do the job, but no firm judgment can be made until the question has been subjected to more searching examination by the Congress.

c. While providing the largest amount of dollar reductions to individuals, we believe that a reform of tax rates to remove impediments to growth and job-creating investment—as contrasted to tax cut programs designed to inject mass purchasing power into the economy—should provide greater incentives to save and invest than does the administration bill.

d. Consideration should be given to a new approach to provide incentive taxation of growth income. Inasmuch as our objective is growth, many individuals and corporations would be greatly encouraged if, for example, the tax rates were cut with respect to the amount of the annual increase in their income over that of the previous year.

e. We question the prudence of enacting tax cuts to take effect two or three years in the future. In a world characterized chiefly by change, events move too rapidly to recommend such a policy. Although our minds are not closed on this point, we believe enacting tax cuts on a year-to-year basis is the sounder course. Accordingly—depending upon the budgetary situation and the economic outlook—we believe Congress should consider making further rate reductions and structural reforms next year.

f. The tax program must meet the following conditions:

1. Since any tax reduction will further deepen the large and increasing federal budget deficits, the administration must take prompt and effective action —to bring the rapidly rising level of expenditures under firm control in order to minimize the size of the 1964 deficit and attain budget balance in 1965 or, at the latest, 1966.
2. The administration must provide convincing assurances that it will finance the 1964 budget deficit in such a way as not to increase significantly the inflationary potential in the economy.

We believe a bold, balanced, and comprehensive economic program such as we have outlined here offers the best hope of achieving the goals which all Americans share—without exposing the nation to the serious economic risks of the administration's program.

2. Encouraging Savings and Investment

Improving our rate of sustained economic growth depends upon an expansion and improvement of our productive capacity and an increase in our productivity. These advances can in great measure be attained through a greater development of our human resources. In part, however, they depend on stepped-up private investment. We are concerned that the administration's proposals do not go far enough in this key area of removing the impediments to expansion of private investment.

According to Dr. Burns, the reason for recent weakness in this area can be found in the uncertainty and hesitation which has characterized business expectations of the future. This hesitation and uncertainty, he said, has been caused basically by the steady erosion of profit margins and our continuing balance-of-payments deficits and the resulting un-easiness about the strength of the dollar.

Too much attention has been directed to the point that aggregate profit increases have been the highest in our history. Since sales and investment have increased at a greater rate, however, the ratio of profits to sales and investment has been declining.

The profits squeeze has particular relevance to the lag in business investment. Annual rate of profit after taxes on stockholder's equity dropped from an average of 14.1 per cent in 1947-51 to 10.9 per cent in 1952-56, and to 9.4 per cent in the 1957-61 period.

Although the Council agrees that the problem lies in the area of plant and equipment expenditures, it argues that business investment is restrained because of excess plant capacity. As already noted, we believe that most of this excess capacity is obsolete or produces goods for which there is no consumer preference, and in no event is all of it usable.

Moreover, even if we were to grant the administration's primary assumption that our problem is one of inadequate aggregate demand, it would still seem more appropriate to increase aggregate demand in the first instance in the investment sector. Increases in investment demand not only raise aggregate demand: they also raise the ability of the economy to satisfy the aggregate demand.

Specifically, how do we differ with the administration's program as it relates to incentives to save and invest?

The essential source of funds for accelerated investment must be private savings. The administration's combined program of tax reduction and reform—as the majority clearly indicates—is designed almost entirely to promote additional consumer purchasing power on the assumption that it will be translated into consumer demand. Such concentration might reduce the aggregate savings rate in the economy. Yet, it would seem far more appropriate that in an expanding economy, savings rates should increase in order to facilitate the rising investment requirements appropriate to an advancing economy.

Consistent with the objectives of increased availability of savings in the economy, greater emphasis should have been provided in the administration's program on corporate and noncorporate business tax reductions.

Nevertheless, the administration has concentrated almost complete attention on consumer purchasing power and has largely ignored the need for encouragement to job-creating business investment. Imagine the change in incentive and psychology that would occur if corporations were told that they could retain, for example, 60 per cent of their earnings, rather than the present 48 per cent. It seems clear that a reduction of this magnitude would encourage a vast amount of additional investment which would implement the production and distribution of new goods and services for which our people would have a preference if they were available. Similar results would occur if tax rates were substantially reduced for individuals in noncorporate businesses.

3. Federal Spending and Prolonged Budget Deficits

In his testimony before the committee, Dr. Burns said that "the major problem facing the country at the present time is one of limiting the increase in the public debt." Using reasonably conservative assumptions, he predicted that if the President's tax program is approved and if federal expenditures continue to increase as they have in recent years, the budget would not balance until 1972 and the increase in our debt would be about $75 billion over the period.

The administration says that its tax program is the only way to bring the budget into balance, even in periods of prosperity. It is counting on the stimulative effect of tax reductions to result in a higher level of federal revenues than would be experienced without the reductions.

With or without a tax cut, we are in for a long spell of continuing deficits unless firm and determined action is taken to control rapidly rising federal expenditures.

The administration asserts, however, that any reduction in expenditures would offset the stimulative effects of tax reduction. But this is only begging the question upon which we and the administration disagree. Is the primary problem of our economy inadequate demand? If, as we believe and as we have tried to show in these views, the problem is not one of inadequate demand, then the administration's argument against expenditure reform is without merit.

Even if an inadequacy of demand were a major problem, tax cuts accompanied by expenditure reform still would remove impediments to savings and investment, which would serve to release job-creating enterprise.

The reduction and earlier elimination of budget deficits by itself would have salutory psychological and economic effects. It would eliminate the dangerous side effects of financing high federal deficits.

We have heard only words, but have not seen any concrete evidence, that the administration and the Democratic-controlled Congress intend to make any serious effort at expenditure reform.

The fact is that from fiscal 1961 through the estimates for fiscal 1964, the administration will have increased federal spending at an average rate of 7 per cent a year, contrasted to an average annual increase of 2.2 per cent from 1954 through 1960. The huge increases in spending on certain programs in recent years makes this a particularly appropriate time to stop and take stock of where we are and where we may be heading.

Such a review of expenditure policy should concentrate primarily on civilian expenditures where recent increases in outlays have been particularly sharp. But we should not permit any area of spending even defense, to become a "sacred cow."

The administration must recognize that rapidly rising expenditures, just as surely as lagging revenues, can lead to budget deficits and an intensification of our debt management problems. These are difficult and important problems, which the administration has failed to discuss.

Two questions must be considered: (1) How will the budget deficits be financed? and (2) What effects will the financing of these deficits have on interest rates, on the level of private investments, and on prices?

With respect to the first question, if the deficit is largely financed out of savings, with the new government securities sold to individuals and nonbanking institutions, such as insurance companies, the effect would be an increase in interest rates above what they would have been without the federal deficit. The reason for this is that the non-government demand for loanable funds is likely to remain relatively constant or increase. However, a new demand for loanable funds is created when the government enters the financial markets and borrows to finance the new deficits. As a result, the prices of government securities—and ultimately all securities—must be driven down and the interest rates must correspondingly rise.

To the extent that interest rates rise as a result of deficit financing, an element of business costs—as well as government costs—have been increased. The same conclusion holds true with respect to financing of consumer purchases. To the extent that interest rates on consumer borrowing are raised, the real income of consumers is lowered.

More important, however, is the effect of higher interest rates in discouraging private investment. Since a rapid rate of economic growth requires a high level of private investment, growth is slowed when high interest rates deter investment and when savings are drawn off to finance federal deficits rather than investment.

Alternatively, what are the effects from that portion of additional government debt financed from banking institutions? Here the answer depends on the actions of the monetary authorities. If the monetary authorities place an absolute limit on the amount of total banking reserves, then commercial banks are in exactly the same position as nonbank lenders, i.e., the amount of their total lending has not been changed even though a new demand for loanable funds has been created. The result in this instance must be exactly the same as in the case of government borrowing from nonbank institutions.

However, if the monetary authorities permit an increase in reserves, the banking system can simply create the additional funds necessary to finance the new federal deficits. The administration apparently has assumed this situation, but it has neglected to mention that newly created "money," whatever the amount or purpose, is just so much added to the inflationary potential. The administration argues further that "no inflationary problems should arise so long as there is unemployment and capacity available to produce additional goods and services." This is not necessarily true because the increased demands of individuals and businesses may be for goods and services where excess capacity and trained manpower do not exist, which an analysis of our present situation reveals is the case. Further, if the additional demand raises prices and costs in these areas, there may be a "spillover" effect toward increasing costs and some prices throughout the economy. Hence, some price rises may be expected even with unused resources in the economy.

The dangers and injustices caused even by modest doses of inflation were highlighted by the majority of the Joint Economic Committee in its 1960 report on "Employment, Growth, and Price Levels." In that report, the majority said:

The acceptance of continuing increases, even though quite modest, in the general level of prices may result in acceleration of the inflationary pressures and lead to economic instability.

Inflation is unjust. This is true whether it creeps or gallops. It redistributes income and wealth according to the ability of people to protect themselves against its effects. Because of this it benefits the strong at the expense of the weak. The avoidance of inflation, therefore, is an important goal of economic policy.

We are tempted to underscore for the benefit of the present administration this good advice from the Democratic majority of this committee two years ago.

For the reasons stated above, and because of the balance-of-payments and gold outflow considerations, we believe that tax cuts without expenditure control would create real and possibly permanent economic damage. We do not suggest an across-the-board nor a dollar-for-dollar cut in federal expenditures. In view of the nation's present domestic needs and international and security commitments—and the administration's political commitments—such an approach would be unrealistic.

What we do seek, however, is a reform of federal expenditure policy to effect important savings, without impairing the national security, and which would stimulate rather than retard economic growth. Indeed, thoughtful and selective control of, and judgment in, determining federal expenditures—with prudent establishment of national priorities—can increase our national security and remove impediments to our economic growth.

LET US BEGIN: AN INVITATION
TO ACTION ON POVERTY

John Kenneth Galbraith

In addition to the opponents who thought that the federal expenditures should be cut before taxes were reduced, the Kennedy tax proposals were also opposed by those who thought that the country needed more public expenditures. They were not against fiscal stimulus but argued that it should be provided by public expenditures that would meet public needs as well as stimulate aggregate demand. They worried about the precedent that a tax reduction would set and argued that when fiscal policies were needed to deflate the economy tax increases would be very difficult to achieve. Professor Galbraith presents the case for more public expenditures and points out the dangers involved in a tax reduction. John Kenneth Galbraith is a Professor of Economics at Harvard University.

The misfortune of the liberal is that he must suffer the censure of both his friends and his enemies. His friends are particularly severe, for, naturally enough, they hold him to much higher standards of intellectual deportment than those with whom they disagree. I speak here from experience. Because, a few years ago, I wrote a book which described our society as affluent I have ever since been accused of believing that there are no poor people left in the United States. This charge comes, to be sure, from those who have not read the book but as every author is aware this accounts for a distressingly large majority of the voting population and a not insignificant fraction of the more eloquent critics. I continue to hope that those who have been more profligate of their energy will recall that one of my principal purposes was to urge that growing wealth would not, of itself, solve the problem of poverty. Instead, with increased well-being, the position of those left behind would become ever more shameful—an anachronism from which we would be able to divert our eyes only with ever-increasing determination. But my purpose here is not to defend myself but—in the deeper tradition of American liberalism—to dwell on the shortcomings of other people.

The problem of poverty in the United States is the problem of people who for reasons of location, education, health, environment in youth or mental deficiency, or race are not able to participate effectively—or at all—in the economic life of the nation. Being barred from participation they are denied the income that accrues to participants. So they live in deprivation.

Those who argue that a steady expansion in economic output is a necessary condition for the elimination of poverty have a valid case. People who are able to participate in the economy must have a chance for jobs. And there also continues to be good reason for seeking a broad and equitable distribution of the revenues from production. Despite considerable propaganda to the contrary, our greatest current need is not a decision to be tender to the well-to-do. Their situation is not nearly so desperate as popularly represented or the current congressional desire to help the higher tax brackets would seem to suggest. We should continue to bear in mind that one makes an economy work not by rewarding the rich but by rewarding all who contribute to its success.

But on one elementary point there must be no doubt. If the head of a family is stranded deep on the Cumberland Plateau, or if he never went to school, or if he has no useful skill, or if his health is broken, or if he succumbed as a youngster to a slum environment, or if opportunity is denied to him because he is a Negro, then he will be poor and his family will be poor and that will be true no matter how opulent everyone else becomes. A very large part of the very worst poverty is the affliction of people who are unable to make a useful contribution to the economy. Being unable to contribute they receive nothing. They will continue to receive nothing no matter how rapidly the economy expands.

Equally there must be no doubt that the means for rescuing these people or their children—investment to conserve and develop resources, assistance in relocation of workers, assistance to new industries, vastly improved education, training and retraining, medical and mental care, youth employment, counseling, urban recreational facilities, housing, slum abatement, and the assurance of full civic equality—will require public effort and public funds. This must be honest effort and not pilot projects which are a modern device for simulating action without spending money. Poverty can be made to disappear. It won't be accomplished simply by stepping up the growth rate any more than it will be accomplished by incantation or ritualistic washing of the feet. Growth is only for those who can take advantage of it.

We have, of course, no hope of erasing this blot on our social life if we are affected by the thinking of that new and interesting cult which call themselves the modern conservatives. As to this, I suppose, there will be general agreement. The modern conservative is not even especially modern. He is engaged on the contrary, in one of man's oldest, best financed, most applauded, and, on the whole, least successful exercises in moral philosophy. That is the search for a superior moral justification for selfishness. It is an exercise which always involves a certain number of internal contradictions and even a few absurdities. The conspicuously wealthy turn up urging the character-building value of privation for the poor. The man who has struck it rich in minerals, oil, or other bounties of nature is found explaining the debilitating effect of unearned income from the state. The corporation executive who is a superlative success as an organization man weighs in on the evils of bureaucracy. Federal aid to education is feared by those who live in suburbs that could easily forgo this danger, and by people whose children are in private schools. Socialized medicine is condemned by men emerging from Walter Reed Hospital. Social Security is viewed with alarm by those who have the comfortable cushion of an inherited income. Those who are immediately threatened by public efforts to meet their needs—whether widows, small farmers, hospitalized veterans, or the unemployed—are almost always oblivious to their danger.

The first three or four times that I read *The Conscience of a Conservative* I confess that I was slightly attracted by the vision of a young two-fisted man of my own age, up from the ranks, self-reliant, self-made, accepting the risk of illness without income, disdaining any organized provision for his old age, asking only that he might keep safe from the tax collector what he earned by the sweat of his own brow. I continue to think of this as the work of a detached scholar. But, in the purely literary way that one writer explores the psyche of another, I wonder if some personal anxieties are not eased by identification with a really good department store.

I have no thought of reproach here. My own interest in the Harvard retirement plan slumped appallingly when my books began to appear on the best-seller lists and my wife, quite unexpectedly, became the beneficiary of the small remnants of a New England fortune founded, we believe, on the development of a better horse blanket. Why, we wondered, should the Internal Revenue Service share so handsomely in the royalties when it had had no part in the lonely agonies of composition? Should not the spirit of enterprise that produced those blankets be better rewarded in the present generation? For one fleeting moment Young Americans for Freedom had their chance.

It is not conservatives, however, but liberals who are the object of my present interest. It is to them, conservatives will be relieved to realize, that I address my word of reproach.

The elimination of poverty at home and its mitigation abroad are jobs for liberals. They will not be accomplished unless liberalism is a determined faith. That, alas, is what it is ceasing to be. It is coming to be supposed that there is something uncouth about argument, unwise about controversy, and irresponsible about innovation. A high State Department official expressed regret a few weeks ago—I am sorry to say that he had India in mind—that Ambassadors should involve his otherwise placid institution in controversy. Liberals, I fear, are responding to this mood.

I am not at all sure that on either foreign or domestic policy the liberal serves his highest function by acting as a Distant Early Warning system for right-wing criticism. Nor is he most needed in order to provide an elegant and sophisticated rationale for what conservative officials have always done. Nor is it certain that he should measure his success by the applause which the Establishment reserves in really fulsome measure for the once dangerous radical who has shown that he is open to sound conservative persuasion. I am not even certain that we most need liberals in order to alert us to the menace of communism. These are all matters on which I hope to dwell one day at great length. Service to the United States in the field of foreign policy is not without its educational value in these respects. For the moment let me simply say to the liberal who believes that he does enough by endowing the public scene with his presence, rather than by pursuing his convictions, that I agree that it is a good life. It is also a lot like being one of the warriors in the Washington, D.C., parks. The posture is heroic; the sword is held high; but, alas, the movement is nil.*

It is especially important that liberals not be defensive about the public tasks that lie ahead. These are becoming more and not less urgent and it would be an especially shocking miscalculation to postpone needed public services in order to get tax reduction. The case for tax reduction rests on the need to reduce the dampening effect of taxation

* In suggesting that the Purely Decorative Liberal (who may be known for short as a PDL or Piddler) is a waste of time and should be recognized as such, I have no thought of suggesting that working liberals leave the government. This disconcerting interpretation was read into these remarks, I think innocently, by a reporter when I first made them in Washington some weeks ago.

at high levels of output and income and thus insure that these levels are maintained. The further effect, it is argued, will be increased tax revenues from a better functioning economy. Whatever the merits of this case, it provides no support for the contention that needed tasks of government should be held back to facilitate the cut. This is now being suggested and some have gone on to argue that tax reduction is so important a goal that the public-welfare functions should be cut back so that it may be accomplished with safety. Professor Raymond Saulnier, President Eisenhower's informed and by no means obdurately conservative economic adviser, has concluded that the non-defense expenditures of the United States—he mentions as illustrative those for the Rural Electrification Administration, Agency for International Development, Export-Import Bank, Farmers' Home Administration, outlays for civil public works, research—should be cut by two billions if there is to be both tax reduction and provision for the built-in or contractual increases in federal outlays. This means that tax reduction is not for the public good but is imposed at public cost for its own sake.

John F. Kennedy liked to describe himself as a prudent man. And he hated extravagance of any sort—extravagant speech, extravagant gesture, waste of money. President Johnson is, I believe, a wisely prudent man. No one would ask for any other kind of national leader. Departments should answer well for their needs. There is no case for redundant bases, unneeded manpower, or unused services. The quarrel is with those who see in sound public service some danger to society. In fact the public services are one of the two great forces in the fiscal system working for economic equity and social stability.

We have long recognized that the progressive income tax is one such force. In the last quarter of the last century and the first quarter of this century, the concentration of wealth proceeded at a rapid, even appalling, rate in the United States. There seemed to be good ground for the Marxist prediction that this concentration would, in the end, destroy the vitality of capitalism and bring its destruction. The income tax was a major step in arresting this trend and thus annulling Marx's prediction. Conservatives have many reasons to be grateful for the Taft family but there can be little doubt that its greatest single monument is William Howard Taft's successful bid for a constitutional amendment permitting the progressive income tax. I do not share the enthusiasm, now also at a high pitch in some places, for making the tax less progressive. (Provisions in the new tax bill for a more liberal exemption of income in the form of capital gains are a remarkably frank form of free-loading for high-bracket taxpayers. I would hope that all legislators be questioned closely as to their stand on this item next autumn with a view to appropriate reward).

But we need to bear in mind that the incidence of public services is similar to that of the progressive income tax. It also strongly favors the least fortunate.

Thus the well-to-do family can escape to the country. It is the poor who need parks and whose children need swimming pools. Only the poor live in the slums and require the myriad of services that, we may hope, will one day mitigate urban congestion and public squalor. The well-to-do live in communities that have good schools; it is the schools of slum dwellers and wage and salary workers which would be principally improved by federal aid to education. College and universities are more accessible to the rich than to the poor. It is the masses and not the classes who use mass transportation. The elderly couple of less than average income would be the major beneficiary of medicare. Social Security minimum-wages enforcement, youth employment are all most important for the least well-to-do. It is poor children who play in dirty streets. It is their father who gets laid off when public works are suddenly cut back.

Even the protective functions of the state are most important for those in the lower income brackets. Lethal serum and poison drugs do, one gathers, work rather democratically on rich and poor alike. But many of us could probably survive a certain amount of exploitation in our prescriptions, fraud in our food packaging, mendacity in our dental advertising, or thimble-rigging in our securities. We live in parts of cities where epidemics are less likely. The family that struggles to make ends meet, the widow with life-insurance money around loose, the dwellers in urban tenements need the protection of an alert FTC, FDA, SEC, and Public Health Service.

Public services have, to use the economist's word, a strong redistributional effect. And this effect is strongly in favor of those with lower incomes. Those who clamor the loudest for public economy are those for whom public services do the least. Tax reduction that curtails or limits public services has a double effect in comforting the comfortable and afflicting the poor.

This is something which liberals should not forget. I venture to think there is an even stronger lesson for the man of goodwill and good income who, regardless of political disposition, counts himself a good and compassionate citizen. When he is tempted by a crusade against public expenditure, he should remember that the sacrifice is not his. This is all the more true for the crusaders almost invariably exclude defense expenditures, the one large outlay that even the most affluent corporation finds a convenient source of revenue.

In recent times there has been a noticeable reluctance to base social policy on differences in personal income—or even to admit that they exist. Politicians now avoid the subject. As pornography has become ever more popular, inequality has become obscene. Ours is a classless society; we must not set the poor against the rich, or possibly vice versa.

This is great nonsense. There are wide differences in ability to pay in our society. There are also wide differences in the benefit from public services. These are facts of life to be treated without rancor but with full candor. The progressive income tax is a powerful force for equality and the stability of our economic institutions. So are public services. To suppose that public services are of equal benefit to people of all income, and hence that there is equality of sacrifice in curtailment, is to work a fraud on the poorest of our citizens.

My impression is that poverty will be eliminated primarily by energetic action along lines on which we are already working—on civil rights, education, slum abatement, the rest. Action on these several fronts has just been promised, as this goes to press, in the new State of the Union message. President Johnson has put the problem firmly on the public conscience. I would like to urge one further and very concrete step.

To the best of knowledge there is no place in the world where a well-educated population is really poor. If so, let us here in the United States select, beginning next year, the hundred lowest-income counties (or, in the case of urban slums, more limited areas of substantial population and special need) and designate them as special educational districts. These would be equipped (or re-equipped) with a truly excellent and comprehensive school plant, including both primary and secondary schools, transportation, and the best in recreational facilities. The employment on construction in this part of the task would be well-adjusted to the areas of unemployment.

Next, in the manner of the Peace Corps, but with ample pay, an elite body of teachers would be assembled—ready to serve in the most remote areas, tough enough and well-trained enough to take on the worst slums, proud to go to Harlan County or to Harlem. By this one step we would overcome the present difficulty in getting good teachers to go where they are most needed. I would think that the minimum salary for men and women qualifying for this Corps should be around $12,000.

Finally, the scheme should include modest educational grants to families to feed and clothe children for school and to compensate for their earnings. Breakfast should be available for children who need it in addition to lunch. Perhaps there should be an issue of efficient and attractive clothing. Specifically qualified members of the Corps would be available for counseling on home conditions, following up on truancy and delinquency, and otherwise insuring that these youngsters overcome the environment to which the accident of birth committed them. Those who need it would be provided with medical and psychiatric care. The year following, the program would be enlarged and extended to the next 150 or 200 most abysmal areas. It would come to cover as quickly as possible the areas of need. But it would not go beyond areas of low income or, as in the case of the slums, of special educational problems.

This is not federal aid to education. It is an attack on poverty by what I would judge to be the most effective single step that could be taken. Can anyone argue that youngsters with these facilities and this training would share the dismal fate of their parents? As incomes rise above a specified level, the schools would be returned to the localities in accordance with a cost-sharing formula that would take account of increasing ability to pay. Those who fear federal control of education are amply protected. The effort would not affect them.

There are adequate precedents for such action. Some ten years ago it was sadly evident that our highways were heading for trouble. In the richer states they were fairly good. Elsewhere they were too few, too narrow, and too slow. One day soon the vehicles would be backing up into Detroit itself. Then we would have only an interlocked mass of metal full of sound but devoid of movement. The consequences for business would be far from agreeable. Foreseeing this crisis, the federal government stepped in. Disdaining to be bound by the time-honored formulae for sharing costs with the states, it proceeded, subject to some fairly transparent disguises, to contribute up to 90 per cent of the cost of the new highways. General Motors did not object. Ford did not object. Chrysler did not object. The National Association of Manufacturers was acquiescent. Mr. Lucius Clay, the father of the scheme, was at no time stigmatized as a radical promotor of big government. Confident of the same approval, I would urge that we finance in the same way this frontal attack on the areas where education is worst, is needed most, and has the most to offer.

PART III

Restraining Demand

CHECK THE BOOM?

James Tobin

With the Vietnam war and an investment boom, fiscal policy shifted from a policy of stimulating demand to one of restraining demand in 1966, but there were critics that argued that the administration was not being vigorous enough in its deflationary policies. In the early fall of 1966, James Tobin reviewed the state of the American economy and concluded that it was doing very well, that the pressure of demand on capacity was not unreasonably high, that there was no reason to expect a recession in the near future, but that too much of the burden of restraining demand was being placed on monetary policies. He discusses the problem of inflation and its relation to unemployment. James Tobin is a professor of economics at Yale University and a former member of the Council of Economic Advisers.

The United States economy is one of the all-time wonders of the world. In 1966, despite the unwelcome burden of war in Vietnam, U.S. citizens continue to enjoy ever-higher standards of life. Jobs are plentiful and the unemployment rate is down to or below the Kennedy-Johnson target of 4 per cent, which seemed so elusive for so long. The concentration of unemployment in urban ghettos remains critical. But in general, events have proved yesterday's popular economic nightmares—chronic stagnation with growing hordes of "structurally unemployed" victims of automation—to be just as chimerical as economists said they were. Likewise yesterday's anguished complaints of "profit squeeze" have been silenced by routinely fantastic earnings reports and dividends.

Yet the economy is the subject of an anxious vigil, an obsessive search

From "Check the Boom," *The New Republic* (September 3, 1966). Reprinted by permission of *The New Republic*, 1966, Harrison-Blaine of New Jersey, Inc.

for symptoms of disease or even of imminent collapse. A reader of the financial press could easily conclude that the country is in deep economic trouble. He would seldom be reminded that in terms of the real ultimate pay-offs of economic activity—the production and consumption of useful goods and services—we could hardly be doing better.

Why does this prosperity cause such anxiety? There are two main worries. One is the fear that the boom will inevitably lead to severe recession. The other is inflation—the Consumer Price Index, which drifted up at only one percent per year from 1958 to 1964, has risen at nearly 3 per cent a year during the 1965-66 boom. The two sources of concern are related, but I will discuss them in turn.

The first worry demonstrates the persistence and prevalence of business cycle mentality. Most people believe "what goes up must come down" to be a profound but obvious economic truth. Yet 1966 is the sixth year of an uninterrupted economic expansion proving that periodic recessions like those of 1949, 1954, 1958, and 1960 are not inevitable features of American capitalism. In Western Europe and Japan also post-war experience suggests that growth, not fluctuation, is the first law of modern capitalism. The pace of advance may vary from year to year, but actual declines result from very bad policy or very bad luck. The long and successful life of the current American expansion augurs well, not ill, for its future.

However, the character of the expansion did change in the winter of 1965-66. When recovery began in early 1961 there was substantial slack in the economy—workers, machines, and plants idle solely for lack of demand for the products they could make. At the end of 1965 the slack was virtually gone. Meanwhile gross national expenditure on goods and services had increased on average 7 per cent per year, of which one per cent represented price increases and 6 per cent the growth of real output. Of the latter, between 3.5 and 4 per cent reflected the normal growth of the economy's productive capacity—larger population and labor force, new plant, better technology—and the remaining 2 to 2.5 per cent per annum, the gradual elimination of abnormal unemployment and excess capacity. Clearly the 6 per cent rate of growth of output cannot be sustained indefinitely. When no slack is being taken up, when operating and unemployment rates remain constant, then national output can grow no faster than national capacity, i.e., about 4 per cent per year.

Federal policy helped to engineer the 7 per cent per year expansion in demand 1961 through 1965. The makers of economic policy in Washington knew, of course, that some day the growth of demand would have to be slowed down. The question was when and how, especially how to do it without overdoing it. Last winter, just when the economy was approaching the speed zone, demand accelerated. In the last quarter of 1965 and the first quarter of this year, gross national expenditure was increasing at an annual rate of 10 per cent. Much of this was spilling over into price rises, but output was still growing at 6 per cent per year. In 1966 as in the previous five years some of the gains in output are coming from more intense use of the economy's productive resources, though idle resources are harder to find. The problem of smooth transition to growth at a sustainable pace confronts us next year.

Vietnam was one factor in the untimely surge of demand last winter. But quantitatively the increase in defense expenditure has been less important than the boom in private spending for plant and equipment. Investment demand was weak during years of excess capacity, but it has revived dramatically the past two years as businessmen confronted expanding markets that their existing facilities could not serve. Private nonresidential fixed investment now amounts to a record 11 per cent of gross national product.

One of the principal uncertainties about the economy is whether business investment on this scale is sustainable. Are present rates of investment realistically geared to a growing economy and population? If so, investment can be expected to rise along with the economy, though not at the extraordinary 17 per cent per year rate of the last two years. Or does the present investment boom reflect bunching of several years' projects and unrealistic extrapolation of the abnormal 1961-66 growth of sales and profits? If so the current investment boom is transient, and its end, unless skillfully anticipated and offset by monetary and fiscal policy, could trigger another recession.

No one knows, but it seems only prudent to guard against the latter possibility. That is why many academic economists have been urging all year that the 7 per cent tax credit for new investment be temporarily suspended, to provide business with a powerful incentive to postpone new projects until a more opportune time. The tax credit was enacted in 1962, when investment and the economy desperately needed shots in the arm, over the opposition of most of its intended beneficiaries. The situation has reversed, and so has business opinion. The credit has become politically sacrosanct; both business and the administration prefer presidential persuasion as a means of limiting business investment.

Indeed the administration has been unwilling to take any significant fiscal action to check the growth of demand. Since the dizzy pace of the first months of the year has not continued, its wait-and-see policy looks better now than it did last spring. For this respite, the administration owes some thanks to the Federal Reserve (and perhaps to Ralph Nader, too). Never was fiscal policy used more vigorously and effectively to promote recovery to full employment than in 1964-65. Never was monetary policy used more vigorously and effectively to check a boom than in 1966.

In the face of the heavy borrowing demands generated by the investment boom, the Fed has kept a tight rein on the lending capacity of the banking system. The resulting scramble for funds—borrowers seeking loans and banks and other institutions seeking funds to lend to their customers—has raised interest rates to record levels. The competition of the high yields available on savings accounts and bonds has deflated the stock market. Some would-be borrowers are squeezed out; credit is not available to them on terms they can afford. Their spending projects are abandoned or postponed or stretched out.

The main initial impact of tight money is on home-building, although present interest rates and stock values if they continue will no doubt affect eventually other kinds of expenditure too—consumer durables, business investment, state and local capital spending. Meanwhile, since money is extraordinarily tight, the pinch on residential construction is extraordinarily severe. This is unpleasant, and so in a sense is the competitive shake-up of the financial structure accompanying these developments. But populist reflexes are out of place. Now is not the time to excoriate William McChesney Martin or to legislate interest rate ceilings. The Fed is only doing its job, and effective competition for the funds of savers is to be welcomed.

Tight money and the pinch on residential construction are really the result of the failure of the administration and Congress to take fiscal measures to check either business investment or personal consumption. Monetary policy and homebuilding are shouldering as much of the burden of checking inflation as they can—economically, financially, politically. Any further anti-inflationary measures will have to be tax increases.

On the other hand, if a stimulus to demand is needed in 1967 to ward off recession, easing of monetary policy should be the first step and tax reduction should have low priority. The Fed now has all the maneuvering room it could ever need on the side of ease, and this in itself should increase our chances of avoiding serious recession. But the willingness of the Fed to ease money if the expansion falters, will depend on price and balance-of-payments developments. That brings us to the second worry about the prosperity of 1966: inflation.

HOW EVIL IS INFLATION?

As the pressure of demand on the economy's productive resources has increased in 1965 and 1966, so have prices. Although the economy has reached the "interim" goal of 4 per cent unemployment, further demand pressure could reduce unemployment still further, with obvious social and economic gains. But these gains would be "purchased" at the "cost" of more inflation. What is that cost? Should it deter us from aiming monetary and fiscal policy at lower rates on unemployment?

The measure of inflation is highly uncertain. There is really no way to average into a single number the price movements of the vast and ever-changing variety of goods and services in the economy. The indexes commonly used to measure "the price level" and "the purchasing power of the dollar" are compiled with skill, care and consistency; but they are arbitrary and imperfect. Consider the difficulty of evaluating quality improvements and new products. The Consumer Price Index says that the cost of medical services to the consumer has increased 38 per cent in the last ten years. Given the advance of medical knowledge, does a dollar really buy 38 per cent less medical care than it did a decade ago? When the CPI is rising 3 per cent a year we cannot really be sure that the value of a dollar to every consumer—even to the representative consumer whose budget is the source of the commodity weights used in constructing the index—is falling at that rate. Maybe it is falling at 2 per cent, perhaps not at all. But a substantial and persistent change in the rate of increase in the CPI—as from 1 per cent per year in 1958-64 to 3 per cent in 1965-66—undoubtedly signifies a real change in the trend of prices.

Many people regard a general increase in prices as an economic disaster, and some regard any decline in the purchasing power of the currency as a moral default by government. These judgments are extreme. Inflation of itself does not make the country worse off, or better off. The wealth of the nation depends on its natural resources, factories and machines, manpower and skills, science and technology. These are still there whatever happens to prices.

Increases in the prices people pay are offset by increases in the wages, profits, and other incomes they receive. (People complain about the higher prices they pay, not about the higher prices they receive.) A pure inflation—increasing all prices and income, all assets and debts, in the same proportion—would have as little substantive significance as changing from old francs to new or from shillings and pence to decimals.

But in practice inflation is uneven, damaging certain individuals and groups and benefiting others. The losers are those whose incomes and assets are by contract or custom fixed in money value and slow to adjust to price changes. But in appraising their loss remember that the size and security of their incomes often contain some compensation for the risk of inflation. When the bondholder's 6 per cent includes an inflation premium he has little claim on our sympathy when inflation actually occurs.

Inflation is only one of many sources of the redistribution of income and wealth, some anticipated and some not, continually occurring in a dynamic economy. Technological, social and political events are always moving prices and property values up and down in relation to each other, making and destroying fortunes in their wake. Does the government have a greater obligation to possible losers from inflation than to victims of other kinds of economic change? The government has made no commitment to holders of its currency or its debt, much less to owners of private debt denominated in dollars, to maintain the purchasing power of the dollar. A reasonable moral objection could be made to the government's failure to protect or compensate citizens who during World War II bought its U.S. bonds bearing artificially depressed interest rates and found their savings evaporating in the postwar inflation. But the current situation bears no resemblance to that episode.

Nevertheless the government should do more to help people who are not willing or able to protect their savings against inflation by investing in equities or in assets yielding high interest. A way to do so is to offer small savers a U.S. savings bond bearing no interest but if held to maturity escalated in value to a price index or perhaps to the money value of GNP. The government's obligation is accentuated to the extent that it yields to the pressures now upon it to prohibit banks and savings institutions from paying small savers the competitive interest rates on savings available to large and sophisticated investors.

The seemingly perennial U.S. balance-of-payments deficit is commonly cited as a special reason for avoiding inflation at this time. U.S. goods will be more attractive, for Americans and foreigners alike, the lower our prices and costs relative to prices and costs abroad. This makes sense. But the fact is that the U.S. has been improving its competitive position for eight years, thanks to inflation in Europe and elsewhere, yet the payments deficit is still with us. Our trouble is not our trade account, which is probably about as favorable as the mercantilistic interests and policies of other countries will permit. Our trouble is the outflow of capital, and here Europe's relatively faster inflation may very well have hurt rather than helped. An American could gain by buying European properties, watching them appreciate in terms of francs or marks or lire, along with the general inflations in those countries, then later selling and converting the proceeds into dollars to spend at home. The U.S. boom, with heavy demands and high yields for investment funds at home, may help the capital account as much as it hurts the trade balance.

Is inflation the symptom or the disease? Usually people urge correction of conditions giving rise to inflation because they lead to inflation. But conceivably it is these conditions, more than their inflationary symptoms, which are unhealthy. What causes inflation anyway? The literature, popular and professional, abounds with confidently asserted single-cause explanations: too much fiat money, too much government spending, trade unions, monopolies. The world is more complicated. The same explanation will not cover all times, all countries, all inflations; neither ancient Rome nor the Weimar Republic has much relevance to contemporary America.

Inflation may arise from a basic socio-economic disequilibrium: the demands that society makes on its productive resources exceed their capacity. The excessive demands may be expressed not only in public and private spending from current incomes and from savings and credit but also in claims for higher incomes, claims which the unions or businesses or individuals involved have the bargaining power to enforce. Rising prices and wages are the natural response of free markets to excess demand. Some people, those who made their budget plans or their contracts or their collective bargaining agreements without reckoning on rising costs, wind up with less goods and services than they intended to buy. The devil takes the hindmost, and it is only because they are squeezed out of the market that demand is whittled down to match the available supply. But the match is only temporary. The basic disequilibrium is still there. After a round of inflation everything is the same as before except that prices and money incomes are a notch higher. Everyone still has the same demands for goods and services and the same power to enforce his claims by spending money or exacting higher wages or profits. So there has to be another round of inflation, ad infinitum.

Indeed if one believes that people are rational and learn from experience, the inflation generated by a basic disequilibrium must accelerate. People will anticipate the inflation in making spending plans and contracts, and prices will have to race upwards ever faster to squeeze out the excess demand. This is essentially the reasoning behind the orthodox view that there can be no such thing as a creeping inflation for very long; any inflation tends to break into a gallop.

This is also the reasoning underlying the orthodox prescription: remove the basic disequilibrium. After all, a civilized society ought to have the self-discipline and political maturity to adjust explicitly the competing claims on its resources so that they sum to a realistic total. For example, if we load a new defense effort on to an already fully employed economy, we should openly tax ourselves enough to release the needed resources; we should not resort to the capricious and deceptive tax that inflation imposes on the unwary. Likewise if the real wages and profits demanded for producing output add up to more than the output produced, we will have to inject more competition, or alternatively control *à la* guideposts, into the setting of prices and wages.

These conclusions certainly fit whenever the model applies, and there are plenty of examples of inflations that represent the unwillingness of politicians and peoples to face up to the fact that productive resources are limited. But the orthodox Cassandra applies the model too freely and too frequently. Not every period of rising prices represents a deep-seated socio-economic disequilibrium. The industrialized world, especially since World War II, is full of inflationary crawls which vary up and down in speed but do not appear to accelerate into gallops. Evidently there are some circumstances in which a round of inflation is self-stopping; it eliminates rather than renews the circumstances that gave rise to it. And there are other circumstances in which a certain maintained speed of inflation suffices to keep demand in line with supply; ever-growing doses are not necessary.

INFLATION AND UNEMPLOYMENT

In the postwar U.S. economy the range and speed of price increases seem to be related to (a) the pressure of demand on the economy's labor and capital, and (b) the speed with which this pressure is increasing. As for the first, wage and price increases are smaller and less widespread when unemployment of labor is high, when there is considerable excess industrial capacity. The relationship is continuous, not abrupt. There is no magic unemployment rate, no critical threshold that marks the dividing line between inflation and no inflation. Rather there is a broad zone, unemployment rates between, say, 7 and 2 per cent, within which lower unemployment will be continuously associated with higher rates of inflation. Economists refer to this relationship as the

"Phillips curve," after Professor A. W. Phillips of the London School of Economics, who first tried to measure it for England.

Reasons for the Phillips curve are not hard to find. When unemployment is low, unions have more bargaining power, employers have less reasons to resist their demands, and unions or no unions employers have to bid wages up to obtain the workers they need. Experience in the U.S. is not easy to read, but it suggests that to keep money wage rates from rising faster than productivity unemployment must be in excess of 6 per cent of the labor force, with excess industrial capacity correspondingly high.

This is a discouraging conclusion if one interprets any such inflationary tendency as a symptom of a basic disequilibrium—too heavy real claims on the economy's resources—from which an accelerating inflation is bound to arise. But it strains credulity to regard situations of labor surplus and abnormal excess capacity as situations of basic excess demand. Our economy does have an inflationary bias, but it is not due to a systematic excess of society's demands and claims for goods and services over its capacity to produce. More likely it is due to some social institutions, conventions and attitudes that give money wages, other money incomes, and their year-to-year changes significance independent of their real purchasing power. For example, annual advances in money wages and salaries are important for the competitive self-respect of individuals and trade unions. Explicit reduction in wages and salaries are an extreme measure, connoting failure by the recipient or the employer or both. It is much less damaging to pride to accept a decline in real earnings due to the impersonal forces raising the cost of living. Of course wage and salary demands and payments are responsive to the cost of living, too. But the evidence is that they are not fully responsive —if prices rise one per cent per year faster that will make wages rise faster too, but by no means one per cent faster.

The second main factor determining the speed of inflation is the rate at which the pressure of demand on the productive capacity of the economy is increasing. When demand is rising faster than the normal growth of the labor force and of industrial capacity, it takes abnormally large wage and price increases to bring idle labor and plant into operation. Wages and prices rose during the recovery of the thirties, even though massive unemployment and excess capacity remained.

The two factors combined have given the U.S. significantly faster inflation in 1965 and 1966 than in the previous years. The economy is now operating with much smaller margins of unused labor and plant.

Moreover, after four years, 1961-64, in which the growth of demand slowly and gradually whittled away at unemployment, the pressure of demand increased sharply in 1965-66. We cannot yet tell how much of recent price rises to attribute to the first cause and how much to the second. Is it that we are operating the economy at full steam, or that we built up to full steam so fast? Let us hope that the speed of the build-up, rather than the level it has reached, can bear most of the blame; if so the rate of inflation will subside even though present unemployment and operating rates are maintained. Indeed there seems to have been more inflation last winter, when the unemployment rate was rapidly declining, than there has been since, when unemployment has remained steady at the low rates (4 per cent or just below) then reached.

On the other hand, the economy has not yet felt the full impact of this year's boom and inflation on wages. When major labor contracts are reopened next year, the profit and price increases of 1966 will be targets for union negotiators backed by the bargaining power of a tight labor market. However, these wage increases may be more redistributive than inflationary. The abnormally high profit margins that invite them indicate that in many cases they can be absorbed without forcing industry to cut back its scale of operations.

THE GUIDEPOSTS

Organized labor and the administration have been much criticized for violations of the administration's wage guideposts. Certainly many unions have defied them with irresponsibility and impunity. At the same time, the price guideposts called for price cuts in industries where productivity grows faster than average. This precept has been largely ignored, with results for prices and profits that have made it virtually impossible to ask labor to adhere strictly to the wage guideposts. The President's failure to press the auto industry for price cuts opened the way for Walter Reuther's 1964 above-guidepost settlement. Likewise failure to reduce airline fares in 1966 meant that airline shareholders rather than consumers stood to benefit if the machinists respected the wage guidepost. The guideposts were never meant to keep labor and management from bargaining over the division of the pie. They were intended to prevent the management-cum-union of a particular industry from claiming too much—via price increases or failure to make price cuts—from the rest of the economy. This, rather than any numerical wage standard, is the aspect of its voluntary restraint policy the administration will have to emphasize for 1967.

I will list several propositions in summary. (1) The economy is doing very well, and its problems are largely those of success rather than failure. Current inflation does not reflect any deep-seated socio-economic disequilibrium. Creeping inflation is no disaster. Certainly it does much less social harm than the unemployment and stagnation we faced a few years ago. (2) The pressure of demand on capacity is not unreasonably high. Further reduction of unemployment below 4 per cent would be desirable, but it will cause less disruption and inflation if it occurs gradually rather than at the headlong pace of last winter. (3) Demand is now being held in check by an extraordinarily tight and courageous monetary policy, necessitated by the administration's failure to raise taxes. This has overburdened residential construction, and certainly any necessary further restraint—for example, if Vietnam spending increases —should be accomplished by fiscal rather than monetary means. In any case suspension of the 7 per cent tax credit for investment would be a good idea, both to distribute more evenly the anti-inflationary burden now and to strengthen future investment demand. (4) Current prosperity does not doom the economy to recession next year or ever. With good management the recovery of 1961-66 can be transformed into steady growth at a slower sustainable pace. Easing of monetary policy should be the first line of defense against recession.

A SAD PARALLEL OF '57

Paul A. Samuelson

When President Johnson's fiscal policy recommendations in early 1966 did not include either the suspension of the investment tax credit or a general tax increase, the Johnson fiscal policies were challenged as being insufficiently restrictive. Professor Samuelson argues that a 5 per cent tax increase is necessary to halt a mild demand-pull inflation and that the investment tax credit needs to be suspended to prevent an unsustainable investment boom. Paul A. Samuelson is a professor of economics at the Massachusetts Institute of Technology.

By any of the conventional tests, the United States is now experiencing mild demand-pull inflation. The astonishing first-quarter jump in money value of output shows almost a doubling of the rate of over-all price increase.

President Johnson and Gardner Ackley remind me in inflationary 1966 of President Eisenhower and Raymond Saulnier in deflationary 1958, and that is a sad thing to have to say.

In 1957-58 Gen. Eisenhower should have cut taxes; even his old friend Arthur Burns told him that. But Saulnier and Gen. Eisenhower kept hoping for a miracle—that full-employment prosperity would somehow come of its own accord. Well, it didn't.

The second Eisenhower recession did come to an end in the spring of 1958, but it was followed only by a weak and short-lived expansion. The work of—and the credit for—a massive tax cut fell to John Kennedy and Lyndon Johnson many years later. There might be a moral in this for the Republican Party.

Gardner Ackley, good soldier that he is, keeps praying for a miracle. And until the President decides to take the taxing actions called for by economics (both old and new) to cool off demand-pull inflation, what else can poor Dr. Ackley do?

From "A Sad Parallel of '57," *The Washington Post* (April 26, 1966). Reprinted with the permission of *The Washington Post* and Paul A. Samuelson.

Of course, we may get some long-awaited cessation of pressure on food prices, but it is not simply to bring down the price of food or of copper that prudent policy calls for restraint of over-all demand. Why then? Macaulay used to write complacently, "as every scholar knows," but I must write more precisely:

1. As every Ph.D. in economics knows, and as every Congressman must learn, the present level of investment spending is bad because it is unsustainable in the years ahead. Like the 1955-57 burst of spending on plant and equipment, the present burst is likely to be followed in subsequent years by:
   I. Excess capacity.
   II. Low profitability.
   III. Sluggish spending on plant, equipment and inventory. Such stop-and-go capital formation is bad business: bad for the country as well as bad for business.
2. As every Ph.D. in economics knows, when the American economy gets overheated relative to the economies of Germany, France, Britain and Japan, our imports grow beyond our exports and our basic balance of current payments deteriorates. Textbook theory? No; the headlines in each month's financial press.

At the risk of becoming a common scold, I merely repeat for the ears of President Johnson, Secretary Fowler, Assistant Secretary Surrey and any member of the Council of Economic Advisers what all the academic economists have been saying for several months:

1. Suspend that investment tax credit which proffers catnip to the already overfrisky investment cat.
2. Add 5 per cent to all of our tax withholdings and obligations. We ask that you do this to us so that we can do for our country what it can't do for us —namely, spend less on the inadequate supply of consumer goods.
3. Increase the corporate tax rate temporarily from 48 to 50 per cent. It is corporations which are on the investment spree and they will someday thank you for it.

So much for fiscal policy. Meanwhile, back at the Fed, what's been happening?
The conditions of 1966 call for

1. Higher interest rates;
2. Tighter rationing out of credit by lenders;
3. A slower growth in the over-all money supply.

There is only one thing you can say about a professor of economics: he is never satisfied with the Federal Reserve Board. Were Chairman Martin not a philosopher and a gentleman, he might voice complaint that the experts who used to criticize him for being too tight are swinging around to criticize him for being too loose. Yet that's only as it should be, now that the economic winds have clearly changed.

Martin no doubt can now turn the tables on the President and instead of staying on the receiving end of advice can take the offensive at their secret meetings, putting pressure on the President to do the right thing fiscally—raise taxes. But more than nagging is expected from a central banker during times of demand-pull inflation.

In an overtime economy subject to temporary price pressures of considerable magnitude and duration, domestic and international goals for monetary policy finally become reinforcing. The tighter money conditions which will help to dampen down and stretch out the investment boom will also help to lessen the capital deficit in our balance of international payments.

For a month and a half, there has been an artificial easing in the bond market. Martin and the Open Market Committee know how to take care of that pathology. In the immortal words of Adm. Nelson, America—save only for Rep. Wright Patman—expects every Federal Reserve man to do his duty.

POLICY IMPLICATIONS OF EXISTING
INFLATION THEORIES

Charles Schultze

What policies should be used to stop inflation? Both the actual inflation of the mid-1950's and theoretical investigations of the causes of inflation indicate that inflation cannot be eliminated by simply using fiscal policy to equate aggregate demand and aggregate supply. Since wages and prices are less likely to be flexible in a downward than in an upward direction, excess demand in some sectors balanced by deficient demand in other sectors will not lead to a stable price level. When combined with the cost-push types of inflation, aggregate demand techniques may be incapable of eliminating inflation. Charles Schultze is Director of the Bureau of the Budget and a former staff member of the Council of Economic Advisers.

Since those who analyze recent developments in terms of cost-push inflation believe that it would require substantial unemployment to make cost-determined wages and prices flexible they normally conclude that the cost of restraining price increases through the traditional methods of limiting aggregate money demand is too great. Here two variants branch off. There are those, whom we may call the "pulverizers" who would attempt to solve the problem by strengthening the various antitrust laws, applying them, in modified form perhaps, to labor as well as to business. This view implies that by sufficiently vigorous action we can create an economy in which prices and wages behave with the flexibility now ascribed to them by the demand-pull theorists. Indeed, many of the latter would also emphasize the necessity of achieving an even greater demand sensitivity of prices and wages by "pulverizing" existing power structures.

From *Recent Inflation in the United States*, by Charles L. Schultze, Study Paper No. 1, United States Congress, Joint Economic Committee, 1959.

On the other hand there are the Slichterians who feel that the possibility of attaining the requisite price and wage sensitivity is quite small in view of the economic and political facts of life. As a consequence they recommend that we no longer make obeisances in the direction of secular price stability, but face the inevitable and accept creeping inflation. Indeed such inflation is not only necessary, if we are to maintain full employment in the fact or rising costs, but perhaps desirable, as a lubricant on the wheels of progress.

Similarly there are two policy variants among the demand-pull theories. There are some who feel that cost-determined wages and prices are not a problem. Our inflations have always stemmed from excess aggregate demand, which in turn usually arises from overexpansionary monetary and fiscal policies. Control the latter and you can control inflation without sacrificing reasonably full employment. There are some, however, who believe that cost-determined wages and prices have been, in a proximate sense responsible for recent inflation. But the insensitivity of business and union wage-price policies to demand conditions ultimately stems from the knowledge that the government will intervene to assure full employment. A firm policy of maintaining only such a growth in monetary aggregate demand as is necessary to clear the market of full employment output at stable prices would soon teach union and business leaders that any attempt to push up prices and wages will cost them dearly in terms of excess capacity and unemployment. Put more succinctly, the cost of enforcing wage and price flexibility would be only a few sharp recessions. "Admittedly deflationary unemployment is unattractive in itself, but it will serve as a convincing proof of unsound wage policies." One is tempted to call this the "Pavlov technique"; rap the child over the head whenever he eats sweets excessively, and he will soon achieve a positive distaste for candy. How business and labor leaders are to distinguish between price and wage increases which are desirable (and presumably rewardable) for resource allocation purposes, and those which are antisocial (and presumably punishable) one cannot discover.

THE AGGREGATE NATURE OF EXISTING THEORIES

A common characteristic of all of the various types of inflationary processes discussed to date is their aggregate nature. Cost-push inflation is normally discussed in terms of average wage and productivity relationships. Demand-pull inflation is also analyzed as an aggregate phenomenon. Since wages and prices are considered to be flexible with respect to changes in demand, only an aggregate excess demand can lead to inflation.

In the traditional body of economic literature . . . it seems universally to have been concluded that inflation is necessarily the result of a general excess of demand. This conclusion follows understandably from the classical assumption of a perfectly competitive market in which prices and wages are continuously adjusted so as to eliminate any excess demand or excess supply. In such a market, if there is no excess demand (or supply), prices will come to rest; if, therefore, prices are rising cumulatively it can only be because excess demand is constantly tending to reemerge.[1]

A theory of inflation which is based primarily on the flexible nature of prices and wages is not only a demand-oriented theory, it is necessarily an aggregate-oriented theory. Excess demand in some sectors of the economy, balanced by deficient demand in other sectors will indeed result in changes in relative prices and wages, the degree of relative price change depending on the mobility of resources. But an increase in the general price level will not occur in such a situation. Price decreases in the declining demand sectors will offset price increases in excess demand sectors. Further, in such a situation there is no overall excessive demand for factors of production, although the relative demands for, and hence relative prices of different factors may indeed change. Shifts in the composition of demands, within a stable aggregate, thus lead to a change in resource allocation, but not to any movement (except perhaps a temporary one) in the general price level. Prices and wages always move so as to eliminate excess or deficient demands in particular commodity and factor markets.

In the real world, however, prices and wages are not so flexible. In particular wages and prices are much less likely to be flexible in a downward than in an upward direction. This is not to deny any downward flexibility; rather it simply maintains that the degree of excess demand needed to raise prices is significantly less than the degree of deficient demand required to reduce them. There is an upward bias in the general level of prices such that a large change in the composition of demand, even when aggregate demand is not excessive, will lead to a general price rise. The rise in prices will be aggravated by the impact of excess demand in particular sectors of the economy on the prices of raw materials and wage rates. For there is a similar asymmetry in the response of material costs and wages—particularly the latter—to changes

---

[1] United Nations, "World Economic Survey, 1957," p. 5.

in demand. Hence, the absence of excess aggregate demand for factors of production provides no guarantee against an induced rise in the average level of their prices.

Under such circumstances inflation can take place without either an excess aggregate demand or an autonomous cost push. Inflation of this kind originates in excess demand in particular sectors of the economy and spreads via cost increases, to other sectors in which demands are not excessive, and indeed to those in which there is unused capacity and unemployment. The difference between this type of inflationary movement and the aggregate demand-pull and cost-push processes of most existing inflation analysis is not merely an interesting academic refinement. It has important implications for anti-inflationary policy.

SOME IMPLICATIONS

The major part of the rise in the general level of prices during the 1955-57 period we have attributed to two sets of factors.

1. The downward rigidity and cost-oriented nature of prices and wages in most of industry. During a period in which dynamically stable aggregate demand veils a sizable shift in the composition of demand, such market characteristics result in a general rise in the level of prices. The years after 1955 were such a period. Prices rose where demands were excessive and failed to decline elsewhere. Rising prices of materials led to cost increases for industries not faced with excess demands. Wage rates were bid up rapidly in expanding industries, and attracted other wages up to the same levels. Thus the excess demand in the capital goods industries not only led to price increases not balanced by price declines elsewhere, but to general cost increases which forced prices up even where demands were stable or declining. The degree of price increase in various industries was generally associated with the magnitude of the rise in demand, but with an upward bias, so that on the average prices rose, even though on the average demand did not rise excessively. Cost increases tended to be more uniform throughout industry, so that the increase in prices was greater than the rise in costs in rapidly expanding industries and less in stable or declining industries.

2. The attempt to recapture in prices the rise in fixed unit costs which occurred when a vigorous investment boom and a rapid substitution of fixed for variable labor input impinged on a situation of sluggish growth in output. This process was to some extent self-defeating. The rise in *ex ante* gross margins which resulted from the attempt to cover fixed costs at low rates of output itself impeded the rise in output. Had output in the

industries with excess capacity been higher, overhead costs per unit would have increased by a smaller amount. And since even direct labor productivity was positively correlated with production, there is even more reason to believe that a rise in output would have led to somewhat lower unit costs.

None of the foregoing analysis is designed to indicate that all inflations are the result of these processes. Excess aggregate demand has been the basic cause of all of our major inflations. And even the 1955-57 price increase bore the imprint of the influences of the temporary aggregate excess demand of late 1955. But the major thesis of this study has been that the creeping inflation of 1955 to 1957 was different in kind from classical excess demand inflations. Such mild inflation may be expected in a dynamic economy whenever there occur sharp changes in the composition of demand. It is, in effect, a feature of the dynamics of resource allocation where prices and wages tend to be rigid downward. Moreover, these rigidities give a secular upward bias to the price level so long as the major depressions which "broke" the ratchets in the past are avoided in the future.

The conclusions of this analysis with respect to the future possibility of inflation are not so pessimistic as it might appear at first glance. There is an upward bias imparted to the price level by the nature of our price and wage setting mechanisms. But the magnitude of the secular bias is not given by the degree of inflation we faced in the last several years—assuming, of course, that we do not allow classical excess aggregate demand to get started.

1. The magnitude of the shifts in demand between mid-1955 and mid-1957 were unusually great. We should not be continually subject, for example, to a two-year increase in fixed business investment of some 25 per cent (and a much larger rise in order backlogs) accompanied by a 20 per cent decline in residential construction and automobile sales.

2. Rising overhead costs were particularly troublesome because of the nature of the shift in demand. The very fact that it was investment in fixed facilities and overhead labor which expanded rapidly, while other sectors of the economy did not keep pace, was a major source of difficulty from the cost side.

3. The upward price pressure arising out of attempts to recapture fixed costs at reduced "standard volume" is a "one-shot" phenomenon. It is unlikely, indeed impossible, for the average operating rate at which entrepreneurs attempt to recapture fixed costs to continue falling indefinitely. Indeed the very size of the current *ex ante* profit margin, at full utilization of capacity, which resulted from this reduction in standard

volume should become a dampening factor, offsetting price pressures from other sources as output rises toward full utilization of capacity.

We have not attempted in this study to deal with the policy aspects of creeping inflation. Nor shall we do so. However, there are certain obvious implications which are relevant to the formulation of policy.

In the first place, it is quite clear that monetary and fiscal weapons designed to combat inflations stemming from aggregate excess demand are of limited value in situations characterized by the absence of aggregate excess demand. When, as in recent years, prices are rising during a period of growing excess capacity, a further restriction of aggregate demand is more likely to raise costs by reducing productivity than it is to lower costs by reducing wages and profit margins.

Monetary and fiscal policies which do not restrain aggregate demand, but impinge only on the sectors where demand is excessive may indeed limit the inflationary forces during such a period. Between 1955 and 1957 a slower growth in investment demand, coupled with a more even rise in auto and housing demand would undoubtedly have resulted in a smaller price increase and a larger output gain.

The whole question of selective tax and credit controls is far too broad to be discussed here. Their application involves economic and social problems of substantial magnitude. At the same time, however, our analysis does indicate that counterinflationary policy must be designed to take into account the composition as well as the magnitude of excess demand. By using monetary and fiscal policy to prevent excess aggregate demand from emerging we can control one type of inflation. With a dynamically aggregate demand inflation can still arise. Faced with this situation we can either attempt to alter the composition of demand by using selective controls or we can accept the moderate price increases that ensue. This is our choice. We cannot solve the problem, indeed we shall do positive harm, by a further repression of aggregate demand through monetary and fiscal policy.

Creeping inflation is associated with the dynamics of resource allocation. One cannot, simply because it is called inflation, attribute to it all the evil effects of a classical hyperinflation. Like many other aspects of the resource allocation process, it benefits some individuals and harms others. It is, in part, a reflection of the attempt by groups of income recipients to ease the adjustments in relative income status which accompany a change in the use of resources. It probably disturbs the social structure less than do the rapid changes in technology, the shifts in income among industries, and the movement of industry between regions which are continually taking place in a dynamic economy.

EXTENDING THE RECORD OF PROSPERITY

The Council of Economic Advisers

In their 1967 annual report, the Council of Economic Advisers investigated the problems of restraining an economy where demand is threatening to exceed productive capacities. They reviewed the developments since the acceleration in demand in mid-1965, the steps already taken to keep demand under control, and the steps planned for fiscal year 1968. Based on a $12 billion increase in federal purchases of goods and services and the prospects for the other sectors of the economy, the President recommended a 6 per cent surcharge on personal and corporate income tax liabilities to hold the economy at full employment without excessive inflation.

The United States in 1966 enjoyed the benefits of the fullest employment in more than a decade. The unemployment rate reached a thirteen-year low of 3.9 per cent. At that level, demand finally matched supply in most labor markets, a situation which economists define as essentially "full employment."

Real incomes of all major groups registered sizable gains. Expansion continued for the sixth straight year. For the third successive year, growth exceeded 5¼ per cent, a record unparalleled in our postwar experience.

By any standard, then, 1966 was a big year for the economy. Gross national product (GNP) expanded by a record $58 billion in current prices and reached $740 billion. As in the two preceding years, a major advance in business fixed investment was a key expansionary force. And the rising requirements of Vietnam added $10 billion to defense outlays. State and local spending and inventory investment also rose strongly.

As a result, 1966 was in some respects too big a year, especially in the early months. Spurred by the defense buildup, total demand—public

From the *Economic Report of the President together with the Annual Report of the Council of Economic Advisers*, January 1967.

and private—forged ahead at an extraordinarily rapid rate in late 1965 and early 1966. Strains developed in financial markets. Demand outstripped supply in several sectors which were already near full utilization. Many of the new orders simply added to backlogs and put upward pressures on prices. Some of the excess demands were met by imports, reducing the U.S. foreign trade surplus and retarding progress toward equilibrium in the balance of payments. . . .

After years of stimulating demand, policy was called upon to restrain the economy. The need for restraint was recognized at the start of the year. Monetary policy assumed a restrictive stance. In anticipation of large increases in private expenditures and defense outlays, tax policies were applied to curb private demand. In 1964 and 1965, an expansionary tax policy had stimulated the economy; but in March 1966, restrictive tax changes were enacted at the President's request. Excise tax cuts were postponed, and income tax payments were accelerated. Moreover, the President's budget program in January stringently held down nondefense outlays. These measures produced a federal surplus in the national income accounts budget and a net restrictive fiscal impact in the first half of 1966, despite the strong advance in defense spending.

But the magnitude of the task was not fully appreciated at the beginning of 1966. As private demand and Vietnam requirements exceeded forecasts, policy was adjusted to the new developments. Monetary policy tightened further, causing a major cutback in homebuilding. In September, the President proposed additional selective fiscal measures to alleviate excessive demands for funds and for capital goods.

The initial restraining measures, reinforced by the previously enacted rise in payroll taxes, began to take effect in the spring. By the closing months of 1966, it was clear that the brakes had worked. The economy had shouldered the burden of active hostilities without the need for cumbersome and inefficient controls and without losing its basic health and stability. It was shown that policy could work both ways; it could restrain the economy, much as it had been able to provide stimulus during the preceding five years. In particular, the power of tight money as a tool of restraint—as well as its uneven impact—was demonstrated beyond any reasonable doubt.

As 1967 opens, inflationary forces set in motion during the period of overly rapid expansion are still alive, although their strength is waning. But now there is also a renewed challenge to sustain expansion; any further slowdown would be undesirable.

A healthy advance of demand in pace with the growth of potential output would permit gradual restoration of price stability. It would also promote a recovery in our foreign trade balance, thereby aiding the pursuit of equilibrium in the balance of payments. The fiscal program for 1967 is designed to meet these objectives and to assure that the easing of monetary conditions, presently underway, can be extended.

STRAINS AND RESTRAINT IN A SURGING ECONOMY

The major theme of recent economic developments is the continuation of progress. But there is also a secondary theme of problems and imbalances, many of which can be traced back to mid-1965, when the sudden increase in defense requirements for Vietnam led to a marked acceleration in economic activity. By the time measures of fiscal and monetary restraint took hold and slowed down the economy, significant problems had developed—an interruption of price stability, a deterioration in international trade performance, acute pressures in financial markets, and sharply divergent movements among the various sectors of the economy.

The Economy in Mid-1965

As of mid-1965, the economy was advancing steadily and healthily toward full employmant. GNP had risen by $11 billion a quarter, on the average, for the preceding two years; the annual rate of real growth over that period had been 5½ per cent. Unemployment was down to 4½ per cent of the civilian labor force, and the average operating rate of manufacturing capacity was up to 89 per cent. The price record showed few blemishes: average consumer prices in July 1965 were only 6 per cent higher than they had been in early 1961, and prices of nonfood commodities had risen by only 3 per cent. Prices of manufactured finished products at wholesale had advanced by 1 per cent in five years.

Expansionary fiscal policy had contributed actively to the record of 52 months of advance. The reform of depreciation rules and the investment tax credit, both initiated in 1962, encouraged business to expand and modernize plant and equipment. Furthermore, as a result of these measures and the much larger tax reductions granted by the Revenue Act of 1964, both corporate and individual income recipients were enjoying an average reduction of one-fifth in their tax liabilities. Monetary policy continued to meet the credit needs of a brisk expansion and thereby contributed to the relative stability of long-term interest rates that was unusual for a period of rapid economic advance. Meanwhile, federal spending on goods and services was essentially level after mid-1962. As a share of the growing GNP, defense purchases fell steadily from 9.2 per cent in 1962 to a post-Korean low of 7.3 per cent by mid-1965. Defense spending was clearly not the fuel that was propelling the economy toward full employment. But neither was the decline in the defense share permitted to retard the growth of total demand; some economic stimulus was provided by spending on new federal civilian programs, and major reductions in taxes encouraged private spending.

New stimulative policies were being prepared in the spring of 1965 to complete the advance to full employment. Congress enacted a major phased reduction of excise taxes, in line with the President's proposals, and its first stage took effect in June 1965, cutting taxes by $1¾ billion (annual rate). A liberalization of social insurance benefits, designed to help the aged, was enacted to take effect retroactively. The larger benefits were to be financed by a payroll tax increase at the beginning of 1966. Meanwhile, the liberalization of benefits was expected to give the economy a significant stimulus in the fall of 1965 when an anticipated liquidation of steel inventories might otherwise have threatened a slowdown. The retroactive portion, which was disbursed in September, amounted to $900 million. Thereafter, annual benefits were raised by about $2 billion.

Spurt in Economic Activity

The economic environment was significantly changed by the expansion of defense requirements. On July 28, 1965, the President requested additional funds for defense and indicated that further increases would be required in January. Military outlays, at an annual rate, rose by nearly $2 billion a quarter in late 1965 and early 1966. Defense orders expanded very rapidly, spurring demands for labor and inventories by contractors.

Yet the defense buildup itself was not enough to account directly for the acceleration in the over-all economic advance. Rather, it reinforced the previously planned fiscal stimuli and the forward momentum of a strong economy close to full employment. Furthermore, the expansion of defense spending contributed to a significant change in the climate of opinion. The Vietnam buildup virtually assured American businessmen that no economic reverse would occur in the near future. The impact on business attitudes was intensified by unwarranted fears that the Vietnam conflict might have consequences like those of the Korean conflict: direct controls, excess profits taxes, and a huge jump in prices of raw materials.

The increase in defense spending swelled an already strongly rising tide of business investment expenditures. From the second quarter of

1965 to the first quarter of 1966, business spending for new structures and equipment rose by $9 billion. Defense, investment, and social security liberalization, in combination, speeded the growth of disposable income. Consumer spending responded strongly, growing by $29 billion over this three-quarter interval. All in all, GNP advanced at an average of $16 billion a quarter. Real output grew at a phenomenal annual rate of 7.2 per cent, and industrial production rose at an annual rate of 9.7 per cent.

Unemployment fell from 4.7 per cent to 3.8 per cent of the civilian labor force during this period. New orders for durable manufactured goods rose markedly (12 per cent), with orders for electrical machinery (20 per cent) and defense products (19 per cent) increasing especially rapidly.

The surge in demand for goods and labor created pressures on prices in many areas. From October 1965 to July 1966, the annual rate of advance for industrial wholesale prices stepped-up to 3 per cent. Prices of industrial crude materials moved sharply upward—at an annual rate of 8 per cent from October to April. At the consumer level, demand pressures raised prices of services and nonfood commodities and combined with special supply factors in agriculture to push up food prices. All in all, the economy exceeded reasonable speed limits in the period from mid-1965 through the first quarter of 1966.

Moderation in the Pace of Advance

After years of providing stimulus to the economy, policy changed direction at the turn of the year. Monetary policy accounted for a major share of the restraint during most of 1966. The Federal Reserve restrained the growth of credit supply in the face of extremely strong demands for borrowing by business. With intense competition for funds, interest rates rose sharply. Institutions which supply mortgage funds to the homebuilding industry lost deposits both to the commercial banks and to the market for new corporate securities. As a result, residential construction was starved for funds, and the sharp decline in this sector was one of the principal moderating influences during the second half of 1966.

Fiscal policy also responded effectively. Although the special defense costs necessarily swelled federal outlays and were highly stimulative, restrictive actions were taken in other areas. Increases in nondefense purchases were held to $300 million from 1965 to 1966. Several restrictive tax measures were proposed in January 1966, and were enacted in mid-March. These included a reinstatement of some of the earlier excise tax reduction, restoring about $1 billion to the annual rate of Federal revenues; and a system of graduated withholding for individual income taxes that drew off $1½ billion (annual rate) from disposable income beginning in May. These new measures followed the $6 billion increase in payroll taxes that took effect at the start of 1966. In addition, revenues were increased in the spring by unusually large payments on 1965 income tax liabilities.

The national income accounts budget for the federal sector shifted from a deficit at an annual rate of $1¼ billion in the second half of 1965 to a surplus at an annual rate of $3 billion in the first half of 1966.

These monetary and fiscal actions helped to bring the rate of over-all economic expansion in line with the growth of capacity. After the first quarter of 1966, gains in GNP slowed to an average of $12¼ billion a quarter, no longer outstripping the growth of potential GNP. The unemployment rate leveled off, as employment gains essentially matched the growth of the labor force. Manufacturing output actually rose less than the growth of manufacturing capacity, and average operating rates at year-end were below the 91 per cent that had been reached in the first quarter.

The change of pace was first clearly noticeable in the spring. Fiscal restraint appreciably slowed the growth of disposable income in the second quarter and contributed to a marked slowdown in consumer spending. During the summer, consumer demand perked up again. But homebuilding, which had declined moderately in the second quarter, was hit hard by the shortage of mortgage financing and took a sharp plunge, holding down the increase in economic activity.

Business demand for capital goods, on the other hand, continued to expand rapidly during the spring and summer. Although tight money, rising costs of machinery and construction, declining prices of common stock, and appeals for voluntary restraint had moderating effects in particular firms and industries, total business investment forged ahead. In August, both the Commerce-SEC anticipations survey and the National Industrial Conference Board appropriations survey confirmed the vigor of the capital boom. Commercial construction was the only type of business investment that showed weakness; it was restrained by the shortage of mortgage funds.

The capital boom, in fact, was proving too vigorous. In view of the growing backlogs of orders, shortages of certain types of skilled labor, rising prices in capital goods industries, and acute pressures of business credit demands on financial markets, there was a clear need to moderate investment demand. On September 8, the President asked Congress to suspend, until January 1, 1968, the 7 per cent tax credit on investment in machinery and equipment and accelerated depreciation provisions on new buildings. At the same time, he initiated a program to reduce non-defense spending.

The Commerce-SEC survey in November showed that only moderate further increases in plant and equipment spending were planned through the second quarter of 1967. It also revealed that the actual increase in capital outlays in the third quarter was somewhat smaller than the planned advance reported in August; this was the first downward revision of plans in three years. The results of the survey no doubt reflected several factors, including the moderation of economic expansion, the financial pressures on business, and the suspension of the investment tax incentives. Even though orders for machinery and equipment continued to outrun shipments through December, there were favorable prospects that the pressures of excess demand on capital goods industries would be lessened in the months ahead.

Retrospect

Despite the moderation after the first quarter, expansion for 1966 was more rapid than virtually anyone expected at the outset. At the time it was presented last January, the Council's forecast that GNP in 1966 would rise strongly by $46½ billion was somewhat above the typical forecast of private economists. Yet it turned out to be $12 billion too low. In part, the underestimate reflected the difference between the predicted real growth of nearly 5 per cent and the actual rate of 5½ per cent. In addition, the over-all price deflator rose by 3 per cent—about 1 percentage point more than projected.

The primary sources of the underestimate were in federal defense purchases and business fixed investment. While both had been expected to be key sources of strength, they were even stronger than anticipated. As the prospective duration of Vietnam hostilities and the intensity of our military commitment exceeded those assumed in the budget, federal spending for defense in the calendar year ran above last January's estimate by $4 billion. Spurred in part by defense outlays, expenditures on plant and equipment topped the Council's expectations by $2 billion to $3 billion. State and local purchases and inventory investment also were above the projections, while homebuilding and net exports fell below the estimates.

As it became clear that public and private demand was exceeding expectations, the desirability of further increases in taxes came under public discussion. Continuing and careful consideration of this issue within the administration, sharpened by the increasing strain on financial markets, led to the fiscal program of September 8. In retrospect it is clear that, after March, monetary and fiscal policy in combination provided adequate total restraint. It may be debated whether a better balance of demands and policies would have been achieved if a program of additional fiscal restraint had been undertaken earlier in order to relieve the pressure on monetary policy. It may also be argued that the capital boom could have been cooled off sooner if the investment tax credit had been suspended earlier in the year. The question of whether a different timing or different magnitude of fiscal actions might have produced a more favorable balance in 1966 will long interest and challenge analysts of economic policy. But the main lesson is clear from the record: economic policy was used effectively to restrain the economy during 1966, much as it had been used during the preceding five years to stimulate demand.

PROSPECTS AND POLICIES FOR 1967

As 1967 begins, over-all demand is reflecting the restraint of last year's monetary and tax actions. Excessive demand is not now a serious threat. The economy's advance is being stimulated by a continuing rise in federal defense and state and local purchases. In the private sector, significant increases should be registered in consumption. Modest advances are indicated for business fixed investment and for net exports, which reversed a long decline in the fourth quarter of 1966.

Data on housing starts and permits for the closing months of 1966 provide encouraging, although not conclusive, evidence that homebuilding activity has touched bottom. But the recovery of homebuilding will take considerable time, and the effects of last year's monetary restraint will still be felt for many months. Interest rates on securities have declined; but revitalized flows of funds into banks and thrift institutions have just begun. Financial institutions are relaxing their lending policies only gradually as they rebuild liquidity. Interest rates on bank loans and mortgages have not yet reflected the easing in financial markets. Finally, construction expenditures will take place only after contracts are placed and work is initiated.

Inventory investment is bound to be considerably below the unusually high rate in the closing months of 1966. The rate of accumulation in the fourth quarter was about double that required to keep stocks advancing in pace with the trend growth of sales. As in the earlier months of 1966, much of the latest advance in inventories seems to have taken place in goods-in-process held by industries producing defense and business equipment; the buildup may continue but probably at a diminished rate.

Thus, the economy faces a transition to a lower rate of investment in inventories. The strength elsewhere in the economy offers important evidence that the inventory adjustment need not cumulate into an excessive slowdown of activity. The over-all assessment does suggest, however, that private demand is not likely to be particularly buoyant in the first half of 1967 and that a stimulative stabilization policy is appropriate to support steady expansion during this period.

Fiscal Program for 1967

The budget will be appropriately stimulative in the first half of 1967. The annual rate of deficit (national income accounts basis) is expected to be more than $5 billion, compared with a $2½ billion deficit rate in the second half of 1966. Although nondefense spending has been held down, both the special costs of Vietnam and further increases in transfer payments for Medicare will add substantially to federal outlays. Revenues will continue their normal growth in the first half of 1967; but, unlike 1966, no significant net changes in tax payments will result from recent legislation. An increase in payroll taxes of $1½ billion (annual rate), which went into effect at the beginning of 1967, will be nearly offset by the effect of the system of graduated withholding on income tax collections. As a result of this system, which was instituted last May, an additional $1 billion in personal taxes was collected during 1966. Reflecting this, net final payments this spring on personal tax liabilities for 1966 are expected to be correspondingly smaller.

By midyear, construction should be recovering with the stimulus of monetary ease; and inventory investment should be leveling off at a moderate rate. In combination, these two sectors should significantly strengthen over-all private demand. A shift toward restraint in fiscal policy is appropriate at that time to assure that demand does not outrun capacity, that movement toward restoration of price stability is maintained, and that monetary policy does not have to be tightened again.

In line with this set of aims, the President is asking the Congress to enact, as of midyear, a 6 per cent surcharge on personal and corporate income tax liabilities with an exemption for low-income families. The tax will remain in effect for two years or as long as the unusual special

Vietnam costs continue. The form of this proposed temporary tax increase parallels the conclusion of the Subcommittee on Fiscal Policy of the Joint Economic Committee that ". . . a uniform percentage addition to . . . corporate and personal income tax liabilities . . . , to be effective for a stated period, best satisfies criteria for shortrun stabilizing revenue changes." Once fully in effect, the surcharge will drain off an estimated $5.8 billion (annual rate) of private incomes—$3.9 billion from individuals and $1.9 billion from corporations.

On the expenditure side, defense purchases will continue to rise but at a diminishing rate during the course of the year. Transfer payments in the second half of 1967 will exceed the rate in the first half by $4½ billion, reflecting primarily the proposed increase in Social Security benefits. The President is requesting benefit liberalization amounting to $4 billion (annual rate) to begin by midyear, to support the needs of the elderly. The liberalization will be followed by an increase in the payroll tax base at the beginning of 1968. Reflecting the income tax surcharge, normal revenue growth, and increased expenditures, the rate of budget deficit will be reduced to about $3 billion in the second half of the year, and the budget is expected to be approximately in balance in the first half of 1968.

Economic Outlook

With congressional enactment of the President's key fiscal proposals, GNP for 1967 is expected to reach $787 billion, given the $740 billion now estimated for 1966. In the nature of economic forecasting, the projected advance of $47 billion must be viewed as the midpoint of a range of possible outcomes, rather than a precise estimate.

Like any quantitative forecast, the estimated rise of $47 billion is meant to convey important qualitative judgments. The advance will be considerably less rapid than the record increase of $58 billion in GNP in 1966. Healthy forward motion will nevertheless be maintained. Real output should expand nearly in line with the 4 per cent growth of potential. . . . The price record should improve; over-all prices may increase slightly more than 2½ per cent. Finally and most important, the nation should continue to experience substantially full employment in 1967. The unemployment rate should be essentially the same as in 1966, when it averaged 3.9 per cent. After allowance for an increase of more than 300,000 in the Armed Forces, the civilian labor force should expand by about 1¼ million, and civilian employment should approximately keep pace.

Outlook by Sectors

A more balanced composition of output is expected in 1967, reflecting the aims and effects of policy. Neither business fixed investment nor inventory investment will, or should, be strong stimulating forces. On the other hand, housing should gain as the year develops, and defense outlays will continue to provide economic stimulus.

Business Fixed Investment. After increasing by an average of 13½ per cent annually over the past three years, business fixed investment should expand much more slowly in 1967. Evidence of this is already provided in the November survey of intentions for plant and equipment spending. Investment should increase only slightly from its level in the fourth quarter of 1966, and should show a rise of about $3 billion from 1966 to 1967. This pace would be a welcome respite, permitting pressures on capital goods industries to abate. The ratio of business investment to GNP should decline slowly to a more sustainable level near 10¼ per cent by year end.

Business Inventories. Inventory investment was at a record high last year, partly because of the rise in goods-in-process stocks of industries producing business and defense equipment. Any further buildup of these stocks will be small. Stocks in most areas are expected to rise in line with steady and moderate advances in sales. Inventory investment for 1967 may be about half the $11½ billion rate experienced in 1966. Most of the decline to a sustainable rate should occur in the first half of the year, with a leveling off thereafter.

Homebuilding. As monetary policy continues to ease, housing starts should begin to rise above their current depressed level. Additional help should come from actions of the Federal Home Loan Bank Board (FHLBB) and the Federal National Mortgage Association (FNMA). Because of the lag between mortgage commitments and construction expenditures, activity should begin to increase very gradually in the first half of the year and gain considerable momentum in the latter part. Demographic factors and low vacancy rates point to latent strength in homebuilding, which should become evident during the course of 1967.

Residential construction expenditures are expected to increase by about $5 billion to $6 billion from the fourth quarter of 1966 to the fourth quarter of 1967. Even so, for the year as a whole, they would still be about $1 billion below the 1966 average.

Government. State and local government purchases, which grew by 10 per cent, or $7 billion in 1966, should expand in 1967 by about $8 billion in response to growing needs and strongly increasing revenues. The increase in federal purchases from 1966 to 1967 is expected to be $12 billion, mostly for defense. But the rate of advance will taper off during the course of the year.

Net Exports. As the growth of imports moderates and exports show strength, net exports should expand throughout the year, rising about $1 billion from 1966 to 1967.

Consumption. The fiscal program for 1967 will have a direct impact on after-tax incomes of households and thus on their consumption outlays. The growth in transfer payments will increase disposable income, while the proposed surtax on individual incomes and the payroll tax that just took effect will restrain it. The more moderate growth expected in employment and the net effect of these policy measures will hold the growth of disposable personal income in 1967 somewhat below the gain in 1966.

This advance in disposable income should make possible a gain in consumption of more than $30 billion in 1967, compared with a rise of $33½ billion in 1966. In real terms, the expected gains in consumption and disposable income in 1967 are expected approximately to match those of 1966. The saving rate in 1967 should remain close to the 1966 level of 5¼ per cent, a little below the average of recent years.

Flexibility

The program and the outlook for 1967 provide good prospects for a growth of demand that keeps pace with capacity. But the experience of 1966 is a clear reminder that surprises can develop and that policy must be alert to them. This year, the risks are on both sides: demand could grow too sluggishly or too strongly. A balance of risks is a necessary feature of a full employment economy moving ahead essentially in line with potential.

In the first half of 1967, there are forces which could make for sluggish private demand, but a sizable stimulus from fiscal policy will help to clear the hurdles. Then, in the second half, housing should move up strongly, the rate of inventory investment should stop declining, and transfer payments will rise. Indeed, with these developments, private demand could once again move ahead rapidly, perhaps even too rapidly. But, by that time, the President's tax program will be moderating the advance.

At any time in the year, the outlook for plant and equipment demand could be upset if the recent signs of moderation should prove illusory or if a sharp and pronounced decline should occur. Either development could call for a response by stabilization policies.

Cessation of hostilities in Vietnam would be the most welcome surprise that could develop in 1967. It would challenge economic policy to smooth the transition—and policy will be ready to meet the challenge. On the other hand, an unexpected increase in outlays required for defense would have important consequences, pointing toward further measures of restraint, particularly from fiscal policy.

A firm set of attainable objectives, a program that fits the present outlook, alertness to changing circumstances, and flexible and well-coordinated use of policy instruments are the necessary means for maintaining full employment and achieving a sustainable advance in 1967.

IMPROVING STABILIZATION TOOLS OVER THE LONG RUN

The tools of economic stabilization now at our disposal can cope quite effectively with the problems that lie immediately ahead. Over the coming years, however, there is a continuing need to sharpen and improve these policy tools—as well as the institutional framework within which they operate—so that short-term policy can respond efficiently and flexibly to economic fluctuations and simultaneously promote progress along a path of sustainable long-term growth.

Uses of Monetary Policy

As a stabilization tool, monetary policy has some distinct advantages. Policy changes can be made quickly in response to changing signals. Furthermore, as was evident in 1966, a restrictive monetary policy can reduce aggregate demand fairly promptly and very sharply.

But there are also distinct limitations on the uses of monetary policy. As demonstrated in 1966 its impact on different sectors of the economy can be highly uneven, both in magnitude and in timing. Moreover, if monetary policy is used repeatedly and in large doses to restrain inflation, it may be difficult to avoid a long-term upward trend in interest rates. And the scope for monetary policy may at times also be limited by balance of payments considerations.

The uneven impact of changes in credit conditions is unavoidable to a certain extent. Monetary policy inevitably has its principal effect on those sectors that are particularly dependent on credit. But the special vulnerability of some sectors to tightening is also importantly related to certain structural characteristics of our financial institutions. Over time, there should be scope for reducing the uneven impact of monetary policy through various modifications in these institutional arrangements. This is particularly true with respect to homebuilding.

In the postwar period, changing monetary conditions have contributed to several major swings in residential construction. This particularly sensitive reaction to monetary conditions reflects the reliance of mortgage financing on institutional rather than open market sources of credit and its special reliance on one particular type of institution, namely savings and loan associations. The most recent example of this sensitivity was in 1966, when the associations suffered major withdrawals of funds.

There are, however, other possible limitations on the use of monetary policy. There is the danger that under some circumstances, employment of the monetary instrument for short-run stabilization purposes can produce an upward ratcheting of interest rates which could interfere with long-term economic growth.

Indeed, in the postwar period, cyclical movements in rates have been superimposed on a distinct upward rate trend. Every period of business expansion has brought new postwar peaks in interest rates. Of course, rates were abnormally low at the start of the postwar era, reflecting the unusually large liquid balances of businesses and households. But this initial situation cannot explain the continuing upward trend in rates since the mid-1950's. During each period of economic expansion in the 1950's, credit was tightened sharply to restrain demand. The resulting increases in interest rates were not fully offset during the subsequent mild recessions. With each advance, expectations became adjusted to the new level. Rigidities retarded declines, once higher rates were built into the deposit and loan practices of financial institutions.

But an upward ratchet of interest rates is not an inherent or necessary result of a flexible monetary policy. There is now a welcome opportunity for monetary policy to demonstrate its reversibility in a period of prosperity; indeed, that opportunity has already begun to be converted into reality.

A variety of approaches can also be used to reduce some of the obstacles to a flexible use of monetary policy which may be imposed by balance of payments considerations. . . .

Monetary policy is an indispensable tool; and there is important scope for making it more useful. But the measures that can be taken to this end cannot fully overcome its inherent limitations. It needs, and has, a powerful ally in fiscal policy.

Need for Fiscal Flexibility

In any over-all stabilization program, fiscal policy must play a major role. Fiscal policy is generally more even in its impact than monetary policy. Its effects tend to be more readily predictable and less subject to time lags. Fiscal policy, too, can be used with a great deal of flexibility.

In principle, a fiscal program for short-term stabilization can involve adjustment of budget expenditures, of tax rates, or of both. A limited amount of discretionary expenditure variation within a given year can be very useful to deal with unanticipated economic developments. But most economists now agree that the selection of appropriate expenditure levels for various public programs in the budget should be made in light of the relative merits of alternative programs, and of the benefits of added public expenditures, compared with private ones, at the margin. Although the timing of some federal expenditures can be flexibly adjusted, only gradual changes can be made in other programs without compromising their efficiency, at least to a degree. For such reasons, it is preferable to emphasize changes in tax rates (suitably coordinated with changes in monetary policy) for stabilization purposes, and to take full account of the possibilities of tax and monetary adjustments in determining patterns and levels of public expenditures.

A change in tax rates can have a powerful impact; but it usually need not be applied in heavy doses. A large downward adjustment in tax rates was needed in 1964, because fiscal policy had been permitted to tighten unduly over a period of many years. But if active fiscal policy is pursued continuously, only small adjustments in tax rates at any given time should be needed in most peacetime situations. Willingness to consider making such small adjustments frequently would contribute substantially to the effectiveness of stabilization policy and to efficient planning of government programs. Indeed, this willingness seems already established: in each of the past six years, Presidents Kennedy and Johnson have called for significant changes in tax laws. Annual tax changes have, in fact, become the rule rather than the exception.

The very fact that tax rates are less stable than in the past helps to make for a more stable economy. Far from being a source of increased uncertainty—as is sometimes alleged—the flexible and coordinated use of stabilization policies should enable both business firms and individuals to make their economic decisions in a climate of greater confidence. A knowledge that policies are alert to changing developments should help to reduce the important uncertainties about possible fluctuations in sales, profits, and employment opportunities.

PART IV

Future Fiscal Needs

THE FUTURE OF OUR FISCAL SYSTEM

Walter W. Heller

What problems will fiscal policy face in the next five to ten years if the economy is able to return to peace-time conditions with the end of the war in Vietnam? Walter W. Heller argues that in the long run the problem is not restraining demand but offsetting fiscal drag so that the economy can grow at its full employment potential. He argues that increased civilian expenditures, higher transfer payments to state and local governments, and tax reductions all have a role to play as part of the fiscal dividend provided by a revenue system that generates a rising full employment surplus. Walter W. Heller is a former Chairman of the Council of Economic Advisers (1961-1964) and is currently a professor of economics at the University of Minnesota.

As we tackle the fiscal issues that now confront us, we can draw on some rather impressive gains achieved in recent years.

First, we have the demonstrated success of the 1964 tax cut which symbolizes the shift from an antirecession, shock-absorbing fiscal policy to a gap-closing, economic-propulsion policy. ("Business Week" said this of the tax cut recently: "It isn't often that the U.S. can look back on a major change in government policy and find absolutely no grounds for criticism.")

Second, we have a general growth of confidence in the ability of economists to estimate the U.S. economy's potential and its performance gap, its growth rate, its income-consumption and demand-unemployment relations, matched, in part, by a growth in economists' confidence in

From "The Future of our Fiscal System," *Journal of Business* (July 1965). Reprinted from "The Future of our Fiscal System" by Walter W. Heller from the *Journal of Business* by permission of the University of Chicago Press. Copyright 1965 by the University of Chicago.

themselves. We see this confidence increasingly founded on the test of performance on the policy firing line. (Note that I do not extend my claim to cover GNP forecasting.)

Third, we have a growing acceptance of the essential role of government in influencing the level of demand through positive fiscal and monetary policies, a recognition that this can be done without destroying, endangering, or in any way limiting individual freedom of choice—and we have the resulting development of a closer government-business partnership.

Fourth, we have seen an ebbing of the fears that so often in the past caused our economic policy "to be sicklied o'er with the pale cast of inaction": the fear that budget deficits necessarily spell inflation, insolvency, and irresponsibility; the fear that a growing national debt would burden our children and grandchildren and bring on national bankruptcy (even though it has shrunk from 116 per cent of GNP in 1947 to under 50 per cent today); the fear that fiscal planning, however prudent, necessarily spells growing centralization of power in Washington.

These advances give us guidance and encouragement in coping with our future fiscal problems—but they do not solve those problems for us. Although we have moved steadily and strongly toward fuller resource utilization and faster growth without any of the inflation, the structural bottlenecks, and the excesses feared by men of little faith in the power and resiliency of the American economy, these problems remain:

1. We face a vast inpouring of new labor, new plant capacity and new technology that must be matched with rising demand.

2. We have a fiscal system that generates such fast-growing revenues at the federal level that our economic health is threatened by a recurring "fiscal drag" and such slow-growing revenues (relative to needs) at the state-local level that our political health is threatened by a recurring fiscal lag.

3. We may well find that today's mix of consumption and investment stimulus, of tax cuts and spending increase, of payroll-tax increases and income-tax cuts does not fit tomorrow's economic needs—nor tomorrow's citizen preferences.

4. We have much yet to do to free our tax structure—and especially our income tax—of its impediments to an efficient flow of capital, its unlike treatment of like incomes, and its excessive burdens on small incomes.

5. We have yet to gear both our tax legislative process and our executive spending process (including, in part, our social security system) to the swift actions and shifts that may be needed to deal with surprises in an

imperfect economic world—and, in particular, to forestall recessions or nip them in the bud.

If this list of unfinished and recurring business seems to write a rough agenda for my comments, it is meant to.

THE FEDERAL FISCAL BALANCE

Bitter experience shows that there is nothing easier than letting the full employment surplus grow. Time, bringing with it ever increasing productivity and rapid additions of young new workers to the labor force (the labor force will rise from over 77 million today to 86 million by 1970 and 101 million by 1980), will rapidly raise the full-employment surplus unless deliberate and repeated steps are taken to prevent it.

The situation, in short, is decidedly asymmetric—time works against the correction of overly restrictive plans and for the correction of overly stimulative ones.

Whether budget balance at full employment, rather than a deficit or surplus, will continue to be the right policy target in the years ahead, I am not prepared to say. I do not believe that proper policy-making forces us to decide now which is the right target for later years. Waiting will provide much of the information that analysis can at best approximate.

Thus, by 1968 we will be in a much better position to assess the strength of investment demand for 1969 and 1970 than we are now. We will also know by then whether the better balance-of-payments situation we expect will, in fact, materialize—and thereby give us greater freedom to choose, if we wish, an easier monetary policy, combined with a tighter budget policy. And we will know whether the maturing of our postwar baby crop will boost our propensity to consume.

FISCAL DRAG AND FISCAL DIVIDENDS

Present programs have eliminated the full-employment surplus. But in the future, it will again and again rear its ugly head in the form of a growing fiscal drag, or its lovely head in the form of recurring fiscal dividends. I refer here, of course, to the automatic growth of federal revenues, not to such occasional jolts as the prospective rise of payroll taxes by $5 billion a year next January 1.

The crux of the matter is that, at existing federal tax rates, our

normal economic growth of about 4 per cent a year in real terms—about
5.5 per cent in current prices—currently generates added cash receipts
of about $7 billion a year, rising to nearly $9 billion a year by the end
of the decade. Of this amount, perhaps $1.5 billion today and nearly
$2 billion a year by 1970 will be absorbed by the roughly 6 per cent
annual growth in social security benefits under existing programs. So
we are dealing, on an administrative budget basis, with an average automatic growth of over $6 billion a year in federal revenues.

Existing tax rates would produce nearly $35 billion more in revenue
in 1970 than they do today. Apart from the debt retirement that will
become appropriate if demand strains our productive resources, this
huge growth will enable us to declare generous dividends in the form of:
support for vital new or expanded federal programs; well-timed tax
cuts; more generous transfers of funds to hard-pressed state and local
governments; perhaps even a helping hand to the social security system.

The choices we make among these alternatives will profoundly affect
the future of our fiscal system.

Expenditures

I start with the basic assumption that added civilian expenditures will
absorb perhaps half of the automatic increase in revenue—or some-
where between $15 and $20 billion of the $35 billion available to us
between now and 1970. My figure is based partly on a projection of the
past increases in civilian expenditures—outlays for purposes other than
defense and space have risen by an average of about $2 billion annually
whether measured from 1953 or 1960 to the present. To this I add an
allowance for the pickup in tempo implicit in the programs for the Great
Society. (It is worthwhile noting that even with a $3 billion annual
increase, or roughly 3 per cent annually, federal expenditures would
continue to decline as a percentage of GNP, having already declined
from 17.2 per cent in fiscal year 1959 to an estimated 15.2 per cent in
fiscal year 1965 on an administrative budget basis and from 20.3 per
cent to 19.0 per cent on a cash basis.)

But I will not take refuge in mere projections. The polluted air I
breathe in many large cities, the polluted Lake Michigan and Puget
Sound beaches where I swam as a boy, progressive urban decay, the
blight of human poverty amidst plenty, the vanishing wilderness, the
uneven struggle between beauty and ugliness in American life, the
excessive incidence of illiteracy, crime, and delinquency—not to mention more mundane things like the flooding Minnesota and Mississippi

rivers and the bumps and potholes in Minneapolis streets—all these reach out for a larger share of that $6 billion-plus annual dividend, either by direct programs or by more generous transfers to state-local government.

How else are we going to gain control of our public environment rather than let it control us in a "half-finished society," to use the graphic phrases of Faltermayer? How else can we make progress toward a society that will not only be large and productive but great and good?

But the matter goes beyond your value preferences and mine. It asks also whether our growth targets require that we put more of our savings into public investments—both in intangible investments in education, research and development, and technological advance and in such tangible investments as atomic energy, urban and regional development, conservation, and other public works. To strike the optimum balance with our increment in private fixed investment—which now appears to be hitting close to 10 per cent of GNP in response to new investment-stimulating policies and higher levels of demand—may well require higher public investment.

Transfers to State-Local Government

And since I have just mentioned the claims of the state and local governments, let me briefly plead their case and, in the process, pose a basic question about the future of our national fiscal systems.

The essence of the problem is a fiscal mismatch: The supply of readily available federal revenue is rising faster than the demands on the federal purse, but the state-local situation is reversed—expenditure demands are rising faster than the readily available revenue supply.

While federal outlays have been rising more slowly than GNP, state-local expenditures rose nearly 9 per cent per year, or almost double the GNP rise from 1953 to 1963. State spending alone rose from $12 billion to $28 billion.

No letup is in sight. The population explosion burdens state-local budgets, not just by the 19 per cent over-all population increase from 1953 to 1963, but by the 40 per cent rise in the five to nineteen age group and by the 29 per cent rise in the over-sixty-five group. Mobility and urbanization call for even more new schools, sewers, roads, parks. Prosperity generates demands for better schools, roads, mental hospitals—faster than it generates new state-local revenues. Price trends, for example, on construction and the services of teachers, have also worked against state-local budgets.

Looking ahead, Joseph A. Pechman of Brookings has projected state-local expenditures at a possible $103 billion in 1970—a 7 per cent growth rate—with receipts (including "normal" growth in federal grants) rising only to $88 billion. This would leave a $15 billion gap to be closed by new state-local tax boosts.

No doubt, state and local bodies can and will do more to tax themselves—for example, states doubled the collections from their own sources between 1953 and 1963. But their handicaps are serious. They face limited jurisdiction, less-than-optimal administrative size, and constitutional barriers. They must also face the problem of interstate competition, the fears of driving out or keeping out industry and wealth. State and local governments also suffer from great disparities in economic and, hence, taxable capacity. Finally, these governments are heavily reliant on tax sources that are not very responsive to economic growth.

Yet the fact remains that many of the functions essential to a great, good, and growing society are carried out by state-local government: education, community development, mental and physical health recreation, welfare—the list is not short.

On simple grounds, then, of redressing the fiscal balance there is much to be said for a more generous allotment of federal funds to the states and localities by methods which will strengthen their independence as well as their capacity to serve their citizens.

But more than that, what kind of a fiscal system do we want? One in which—to put it in extremes—we dismantle the progressive and comparatively equitable federal income taxes while we lean ever more heavily on regressive and comparatively inequitable state-local property, sales, and excise taxes? Or one which relies on fiscally potent income taxes to relieve some of the pressure on our weaker and poorer taxes?

Social Security Support

A similar question arises in relation to social security payroll taxes. How far should we go in further income-tax cuts, side by side with payroll-tax increases which bear most heavily on lower-income groups and on consumption and which increase employers' costs of providing jobs? I do not deny that if these taxes have to be paid to achieve protection against the vicissitudes of old age, unemployment, and ill health, they are indeed a good bargain for those who are protected.

But as leeway develops in the federal tax system, strengthening our system of income maintenance without correspondingly increasing payroll taxes deserves serious consideration as an alternative to deeper income-tax cuts. In particular, a program to strengthen unemployment compensation by tapping the income tax as a revenue source—at the same time tightening unemployment standards to end abuses—has much to recommend it as a means of strengthening the economy and easing burdens on small incomes without boosting business costs.

Tax Cuts

We are paying roughly $17 billion less in income taxes on the 1965 income than we would have without the 1962 and 1964 tax measures, which cut both corporate and individual income taxes by nearly 20 per cent. No such massive cuts are in the cards for the next five years. But even with generous provision for the "dividend claims" already reviewed, the $35 billion potential revenue growth by 1970 leaves room for tax reduction.

I need not dwell on the claims of the tax cutters of the future. They will point out—and rightly so—that tax cuts will boost private demand, vitalize free markets and private incentives, provide added funds for private capital formation, and lubricate further tax reform. To this, I am moved to reply, "I know, I know—yet as a teacher, I can only hope that the tax cut lesson has been learned wisely, but not too well."

The choices among the various forms of fiscal dividends will not be easy. Yet we must remember that:

Unless they are made one way or another, the potential dividends will disappear in economic slack and slowed growth.

They are essentially pleasant choices, aimed not at the lesser evil but at the greater good (to borrow a phrase).

Although they are in part economic choices—because some deliver more stimulus than others, dollar-for-dollar, in achieving full employment and growth—in greater part, the proper mix depends on the country's social and political priorities rather than on its economic priorities.

CHANGES IN TAX STRUCTURE

Some changes in tax structure are implicit in the ways we choose to declare fiscal dividends. And an atmosphere of further federal tax reduction will facilitate other changes in the interest of both equity and economic efficiency. Let me comment on a few issues of tax structure and reform that should command our attention.

Distribution by Type of Tax and Income Size

Our choices among alternative tax forms and alternative burden distributions under the income tax will depend, as we all know, on our equity preferences, our economic objectives, and our appraisal of the effectiveness of various tax measures in achieving them.

Vertical Equity

The Revenue Act of 1964 made a negligible change in the progressivity of the individual income tax. Yet cutting this tax while raising others reduces over-all tax progressivity—and we are not only boosting state-local sales, excise, and property taxes but raising federal employment taxes from 7¼ per cent to 8.7 per cent next year and to a projected 10 per cent by 1970. I see no reason to accelerate this trend by installing a broad-based consumption or value-added tax, as some are proposing, at the federal level.

Indeed, we should be more concerned with the provision of tax relief for low-income taxpayers. Not only has the gradual price creep made our exemption levels inadequate, but rising productivity and rising average standards of living continually raise the level of income which we regard as too small to warrant an income-tax liability, especially in the light of mounting payroll and indirect taxes.

Economic Efficiency

Economic efficiency in taxation is in part a matter of removing unwanted interference with the free and efficient flow of resources. I say "unwanted" because the nation obviously wants to use its tax mechanism to stimulate resource flows into certain uses—for example, philanthropic undertakings, plant and equipment, and home ownership—and is willing to pay subsidies for the favored pursuits at the cost of higher taxes on the non-favored ones.

But these subsidies, like those made through the appropriation process, should be subjected to periodic, if not continuous, review and revision as priorities change.

Secretary Dillon has urged that we adopt constructive realization of capital gains at death to remove a distortion in the efficient flow of investment funds (as well as to gain a fairer sharing of burdens). Again, I fully agree, and Richard Goode has made a persuasive case for deductions of amortization allowances to students for their intangible investments in higher education or vocational training.

Special capital-gains preferences, depletion allowances, and a host of other income-tax differentials also call for continuing review—as to their economic rationale and effectiveness as well as their equity implications. All this is an old story—but worth constant retelling, lest we forget.

A newer story is the shift of national and Democratic policy toward private investment stimulus in response to these inescapable facts of economic life:

1. The pressing need to deepen capital to step up productivity and thereby serve the ends of faster growth, price stability, and international competitiveness;
2. The need to widen capital, to enlarge capacity to accommodate a rising rate of growth of total demand and of our labor supply;
3. In the face of these needs, the post-1957 decline in new, direct private investment from its earlier postwar levels of 10 per cent and 11 per cent of GNP to only 9 per cent of GNP.

My guess is that these and related factors should keep tax policy tilted somewhat toward investment stimulus—of course not neglecting the role of markets as the ultimate incentive for investment—for some time to come. But we should not rule out eventual shifts: We seem to be climbing to the 10 per cent-of-GNP level, as already noted. The Hickman study, for one, suggests that a falling capital-output ratio may weaken full-employment investment demands.

But this study has not yet produced consensus on the rise in productivity of capital goods. Hickman himself considers a range of alternative assumptions about things such as replacement rates and the relative price of capital goods, and the implications for investment demands turn out to be quite sensitive.

Peace time full employment should find investment demands stronger than their trend values. We started from a long period of excess capacity in most industries, during which capital formation had clearly not proceeded at its full-employment rate. As a result, the actual capital stock is further from the desired stock than it would otherwise have been. I do not claim that we should expect to make up all the investment we have missed since the mid-fifties; but neither would I expect to find that the desired full-employment capital stock had been adjusted down to the actual stock through all these years. Also, as already suggested, with labor-force growth accelerating, the share of investment in GNP will be larger than projections from earlier and slower potential growth periods would suggest.

So, I repeat, today's and tomorrow's investment needs continue to call for the more solicitous tax treatment of recent years. But we should keep in mind the possibility that the day-after-tomorrow's economy may again call for tipping the balance, relatively, toward consumption.

Our net assessment of these investment factors will also have obvious and important implications for the size of the full-employment surplus or deficit.

Horizontal Equity

The Revenue Acts of 1962 and 1964 reversed a long unbroken trend toward more and more income-tax preferences. The over-all tax-cut-tax-reform ratio of the 1964 Act is not especially impressive: $745 million of base-tightening revenue increase versus over $10 billion of tax cut. But it was a step in the right direction. And much of the reduction itself contributed to greater equity—$455 million of it in specific measures to improve horizontal equity, while other steps such as splitting the first bracket and cutting the ridiculous top rates also clearly qualify as structural improvements, as does the narrowing of the gap between regular and capital-gains rates.

But we still have a long and tortuous path to travel as the dream of a once-for-all, huge base-tightening in exchange for sharply lower rates seems to have faded.

CONCLUSION

Time and space limitations—and perhaps the obvious nature of what I would recommend—lead me to say little about fiscal measures designed to recession proof the U.S. economy. I do not say that we can, in a single jump, move from a recession-prone to a recession-proof economy. Neither our wisdom nor the state of our economic art (nor, perhaps, our luck) is yet that good. But to make our economy recession repellent is a most reasonable objective. And we should bend every effort, first, to improve the timing of our longer-run expansionary measures, second, to speed up the Congressional tax-cutting process when recession threatens or hits, and third, to speed up the executive-spending process as well.

What encourages me most is that we can get on with the fiscal job in an atmosphere of greater understanding and consensus—of less and less doctrinaire position-taking—than ever before. We may not agree on the precise balance we seek among the different goals of economic policy, nor on the exact blend of policies to get us there. But as long as the proportion of prejudice, misplaced fear, and misunderstanding continues to decline while the proportion of analysis, fact, and comprehension continues to rise, we can be optimistic about the future of our fiscal system and its impact on economic growth and stability.